BASIC CONCEPTS IN CRIMINOLOGY

HANDBOOK FOR LAW ENFORCEMENT PERSONNEL (POLICE, CORRECTIONS AND SECURITY OFFICERS)

ASONGWE N. THOMAS

Order this book online at www.trafford.com
or email orders@trafford.com

Most Trafford titles are also available at major online book retailers.

Printed in the United States of America.

ISBN: 978-1-4907-2700-4 (sc)
ISBN: 978-1-4907-2701-1 (e)

Cover design by Asongwe N. Thomas

Trafford rev.   04/10/2014

 www.trafford.com

North America & international
toll-free: 1 888 232 4444 (USA & Canada)
fax: 812 355 4082

CONTENTS

PART IV

PART V

PART IX

PART X

I dedicate this book to my beloved wife, Na-Nde Susana Asongwe (b. Tanyi) and my very dear senior sister Lem Benedicta Mukah in Agam quarter Bambili for their great motherly love and care for me. May God bless you.

Nubong

ACKNOWLEDGMENT

My appreciation goes to the following personalities who shared their professional expertise, wisdom, and support with me in the realization of this project: Dr. Thurman McClain (author), Department of Education, Washington, DC; Mr. John Wilhour (Accountant) Department of Education, Washington, DC; Mr. Ngongbo Edwin Che, LLM, International Law, database administrator, Titan Corporation, Virginia. Above all, I wish to extend my special gratitude to some two Gendarmerie officers (names unrecalled) of the Tubah Gendarmerie Precinct (NW Region Cameroon) who gave me the initial inspiration in February 2005 to embark on this book project and to write on this subject in particular. In fact this author met them on duty precisely at their traffic control checkpoint at the entrance into the Kejom Ketungo Market some day in February 2005. Kejom Ketungo is a neighboring village to Bambili in Mezam NW Region, Cameroon and located along Cameroon N11 stretch to Ndop. I also want to remember in my appreciation other persons who in one way or the other morally encouraged me to embark on this work. May God bless you all. Thanks.

Nubong T. Asongwe

INTRODUCTION

In fact, in my own little academic world after high school, the word *criminology* was inexistent. I never knew this word, let alone thought of finding out its meaning in my *Oxford Advanced Learner's Dictionary of Current English* (the only reference book that I could afford then), that helped me know the meanings of new words and expressions encountered in my rare reading. I cannot tell with certainty whether the old edition of this dictionary that we used then, carried this word and its meaning or not. Criminology as a social science discipline, is framed from a combination of concepts of sociology, psychology, and law. Remarkably, it is not very popular as a stand-alone subject among disciplines of choice for undergraduate students, or even for those going in for graduate studies. Instead what we notice in most universities' curricula, are related disciplines like Criminal Justice, Criminal Investigation, Crime Scene Investigation, Forensic, Law Enforcement, and so forth. Most universities do not offer it as a stand-alone discipline in their academic curricula, that prospective undergraduate students can read towards obtaining a formal diploma or degree.

From observation, this subject is often pushed to the doctoral preserve. What actually is the reason behind this? Unfortunately, no one has ever taken any interest in this phenomenon, let alone undertake any form of research to explain why this subject is not very popular among disciplines offered for full-fledged college degrees. For this reason, speculations abound. Is the subject matter of criminology so difficult for prospective undergraduate students to comprehend? Or is criminology so limited in scope to be offered for a full-fledged college degree? Why is this discipline so unpopular to prospective college students?

For lack of any supporting empirical statistics, we can postulate the following reasons to explain this phenomenon. Firstly, law enforcement professions and jobs are physically very exhausting and above all, carry a lot of physical risks. As such they are not very attractive to many students. Secondly, the uncanny notoriety of the crime phenomenon, negatively smears criminology as a social science and consequently, renders it unpopular among disciplines of choice for prospective students that would want to further their education beyond high school. Thirdly, the quasi-natural hatred of the law enforcement profession based on the famous "mythical dragon slayer concept"[1] also may explain the unpopular nature of criminology as a subject, since this discipline mostly leads to law enforcement professions. Consequently, low enrolment in this discipline explains why it is not very popular among disciplines offered towards full-fledged undergraduate degrees in colleges or universities.

Remarkably, some junior officers in the law enforcement professions,(Police, Corrections, Security) to whom this subject should be of interest, often show little or no interest in it. Is it because the subject matter is so difficult to comprehend? One cannot conclude with certainty. Far from running down these folks who on a daily basis put their lives on the line for our collective well-being, I am just trying to reflect aloud on why they are not interested in an area of study that directly impacts their professional life. This doubt is the source of my inspiration in writing this book. In *Basic Concepts in Criminology*, I have tried to approach and make this subject much easier and interesting to prospective students of criminology in general, and to law enforcement officers in particular to whom knowledge of criminology is an important professional asset.

My approach is very simple and intended to attract their attention and sustain their interest in the subject. From basic definition of the subject matter, I have attempted to examine and explain some basic crime theories, classical and modern concepts that surround the crime phenomenon, the origin of crimes, classical and scientific perceptions of causes of crimes, different types and categories of crimes, crime analysis, crime prevalence, some control policies and prevention measures, and a few community crime-solutions programs.

This book does not purport to provide sufficient material for advanced students of criminology. As indicated in my title, it provides just an introduction and basic material on this subject for beginners and especially for law enforcement personnel; (Police, Corrections,

---

[1] The mythical dragon-slayer concept contends that the police officer (law enforcer) is of ambivalent nature similar to the dragon slayer who was liked and hated at the same time. The reason being that he that can slay a dangerous animal like the dragon certainly has something of the dragon in his nature and therefore is equally as dangerous as the dragon.

and Security Officers) whose professional performance and well-being are my concern. However, I hope my book will stir and arouse the interest of readers especially law enforcement officers, to whom knowledge of this subject is very professionally relevant. For researchers and other readers interested in getting in-depth knowledge of criminology, I would like to refer them to bookstores and Internet shops where they may find more in-depth material on the subject.

Modern technology has made it easier, and electronic versions of books can be purchased on the Internet and downloaded on home computers, laptops, tablets, Kindles, and other handheld electronic devices very cheaply. For those that may take interest in and may read my book, I say thanks for sharing and wish them God's blessings. Above all I urge them not only to end at reading the book, but to not relent in contributing in whatever way possible (ideas), in finding solutions to crimes or (physically) in combating when and where necessary this nasty crime gangrene that continues to prey on humanity. We cannot afford to let criminals take control of our lives. Thanks.

Nubong

PART I

DEFINITION

a. What Is Criminology?

Webster's new *Collegiate Dictionary*[2] defines criminology as "the branch of science that studies crime as a social phenomenon as well as criminals and the system of punishment of crimes." Controversies in the eighteenth century over the application of punishment for crimes with retributive intentions instead of deterrence and prevention motives, led social scientists to a deeper study of the crime phenomenon. This effort marked the origin of criminology. A century later, social scientists extended their scope of study to include the collection and use of crime statistics, case histories, official records of crimes, and above all, a sociological field approach that involves studying crime incidence; forms, causes, and consequences of crime; as well as social and governmental regulations and reaction to crime. This includes crime types, crime rates, and degree of prevalence within geographic areas or regions.

One prominent branch of criminology is called penology. Penology is defined simply as "the study of punishment of crime and the management of prisons." From a broader perspective, it is concerned with the study of social processes aimed at crime prevention

---

[2]   Merriam Webster; 2000, <u>New Webster's English Dictionary</u>,10th Edition, Springfield USA.

through repression and inhibition of criminal intents with punishment as its main tool. It also encompasses probation (community-based rehabilitation of offenders) and penitentiary science that deals with secure detention and restraining of offenders committed to secure institutions like prisons. Areas of study in penology include prison reforms, prisoner abuse, prisoners' rights, recidivism, deterrence, rehabilitation, retribution, and utilitarianism. Contemporary penology is limited mainly to criminal rehabilitation and prison management. The definition of criminology leads us to a more important question: What is a crime? Before getting into the definition of crime, let us examine the importance of studying criminology.

b. Importance of Criminology

The results of all scientific studies are generally intended for use to improve on society and the lives of citizens. The results of criminological findings are used to enhance criminal justice practices by lawyers and judges in courts, to improve on the performance of law enforcement officials in crime control and prevention, and also corrections (prisons) and probation officials in criminal reformation and rehabilitation. Legislators and scholars also use research findings on Criminology in the formulation of crime prevention and control policies. In fact, criminological findings help these officials to better understand criminals and the effect of punishment and prevention of crimes in the society.

c. What Is a Crime

Webster's Encyclopedic Unabridged Dictionary[3] *of the English Language* defines crime as **"an action or instance of negligence that is deemed injurious to the public welfare or morals, or to the interest of the state and that is legally prohibited."** From *Webster's* definition, we can safely infer two essential components of a crime. A crime is an *act* (action) as well as it can be an *omission* (negligence). *Webster's* definition seemingly is in harmony with criminal law's definition of crime, but falls short of mentioning the other constituent elements of a crime or what jurist professionals call ingredients of crime: "the Intent and the Act or Mens Rea and Actus Reus" respectively. Criminal law defines crime as "an act prohibited by law or failure to act in order to protect the public from harm." This means an *act* or an *omission*. The *intent*

---

[3] Gramercy Books, 1996, <u>Webster's Encyclopedic Unabridged Dictionary of the English Language</u>, New York.

and the *act* are necessary ingredients or elements of a crime and must occur at the same time in order for it to constitute a crime. The *intent* is "the willful and deliberate determination or resolve to commit an act or to fail to perform a legally binding action," while an *act* is "its deliberate or willed performance or failure to perform a legally binding one." As stated above, some crimes do result from omission or failure to act. This is a failure to perform a legally required action or duty. For instance, a parent who fails to provide food to his/her child is guilty of the offense of negligence. It is a legal duty for a parent to cater for the child he/she has brought forth into this world, and such neglect or failure to cater for a helpless child is in violation of the law. Shoplifting, which is the act of taking away an item displayed for sale from a shop without authority or payment and for personal use, is a crime.

Some people often confuse *motive* with *intent*. *Motive* is the reason for performing or failing to perform an act. It is not an element of crime. Motive often drives the intent. For instance, the motive or reason for a hungry child who steals a loaf of bread from a shop is to satisfy his hunger. And it is this need to satisfy his hunger that pushes him to consciously or *intent*ionally steal the loaf of bread. Similarly, it is the motive/reason to look beautiful that may push a young girl to *intent*ionally steal a pair of earrings from a jewelry shop.

PART II

CRIME THEORIES AND CONCEPTS

S ince the inception and evolution of human societies, the crime phenomenon has been and remains a timeless problem that spans across generations. Though so many theories have been developed or advanced on the topic, the causes of crimes seem to be the greatest focal concern of most renowned researches (Flannagan). Unfortunately, any explanation of the concept of crime from its causal perspective is more or less a Herculean task. No amount of theorizing on the root causes of crimes by criminologists, or other social scientists is known to have passed any empirical testing as to win popular acclamation, let alone help in the abatement of crimes. All theoretical formulations on the subject remain simply subjective, if not mere speculations not having any palpable effect on crime control and prevention. A common-sense approach to understanding the causes of crime appears to be the only acceptable method for now (Lilly, Cullen, and Ball 2002).[4]

In spite of its controversial nature and the difficulty in producing any palpable results from the study of the causes of crimes, criminologists, sociologists, and other social scientists and researchers in the natural sciences—for instance, biology—continue to show interest in this ever-plaguing social phenomenon. Basing their claim on empirical findings, biologists affirm that human physiology and the environment predispose subjects to criminality. Meanwhile, sociologists and other social scientists point to an inequitable socioeconomic and political organization of the society as potential root causes or sources of crimes. From a

---

[4]   Lilly, Cullen and Ball; 2002, <u>Criminological Theory;</u> Sage Publications, Thousand Oaks. London

general perspective however, it is believed the causes of crime can be traced to unemployment created by inequitable socioeconomic setup, poor parenting and upbringing, uncontrolled access to modern technology, a dysfunctional criminal justice system, and what some other crime theorists call social disorganization or poor internal political organization of nations. Inasmuch as this assertion may sound plausible, it does not pose as exclusive cause of criminality as we may see in our examination later of other causation theories.

a. Spiritual, Classical, and Positivist

i. Spiritualism Theory (Tannenbaum 1938)

Spiritualist theories traced far back into the Middle Ages and earlier were greatly influenced by Christian doctrine. Believers in this school of thought traced the origin of crime to a conflict between the forces of good and evil spirit embedded in man. The evil spirit is symbolized by demons and the good one by the gods. Criminals were thus considered to be people who were possessed by evil spirits that pushed them into crimes or sins. In this respect, man can either commit a crime or not depending on his ability to resist or succumb to the pressure exerted on his souls by these forces. The universality of the spiritualism theory is very evident. In fact, in the traditional language and culture of the people of the northwest region of Cameroon (West Africa) commonly referred to as "graffi" people, from where this author originates, traces of this concept are still evident. In the Bambili dialect (one of the villages in this region) for instance, the first remark or doubt an onlooker or someone learning of the commission of a violent crime would make is the following: "Laa gang belem ngang mba wo lo?" This remark or question translated into the English language means "Is the man possessed by evil spirits?" This clearly expresses the onlooker's doubt as to whether the culprit was possessed by demons or evil spirits. By extension, people explained natural disasters as punishment for men's wrongdoing. There was also a general belief in the spiritual protection of the innocent. This belief also can be traced in some expressions existing in the Bambili dialect. For instance, a local proverb goes thus: "dizeh leuge mbuh," meaning "The innocent cannot be affected." This proverb underscores or suggests a widely accepted belief that the innocent is divinely protected against any false accusation, curse, or even harm. Hence, he that is punished is doubtlessly guilty of the offense of which he is suspect. As opposed to modern-day concept, crime was viewed as private rather than a collective social issue. Offenders were punished through trial by ordeal or a fight (battle) arranged between the offender and the victim's family. This of course did not guarantee equitable justice as the weaker side, even if it was the victim, remained the loser. Ordeals involved subjecting the accused to life-threatening and of course, painful obstacles as methods of determining guilt or innocence. This idea or practice of subjecting the suspect to an ordeal in order to prove his guilt or innocence in a criminal act is also insinuated in the Bambili language and culture in the following proverbial saying: "nguu[5] gadzwi, beu leuh neboh," meaning "We cannot be speculating on his guilt when there is an ordeal to pass him through." How effective these rudimentary systems of criminal-guilt determination were in those days is beyond any imagination. Whatever the case, the spiritualist concept of crime produced a negative public policy option. It encouraged a jungle lifestyle where the strongest rode roughshod on the weak and went scot-free—survival of the fittest.

ii. The Classical Theory

The classical school of thought on the causes of crime dominated mostly the sixteenth and the seventeenth centuries. It traced the causes of crime to man's nature, unlike the positivist or differential theories that dwelled respectively on the biological structure of man or the socioeconomic conditions that we will examine later in this book. Dwelling on the rational choice and hedonic considerations that influenced crime commission, some of the classics (Bentham [1748-1832] and Beccaria [1738-1794]) viewed the criminal as a very calculative being.

The criminal, they contended, employs a hedonic-type calculus to rationalize on his decision to commit a crime. He usually weighs and balances the risks and the gains and the pains and pleasures that he may derive from committing a criminal act before engaging in it. This notion of rational choice merges with and strengthens the spiritualist concept that the criminal acts on his free will. The commission of crime according to classical theory is not accidental or based on impulse. It involves proper reflection and rationalization in which the criminal usually weighs the advantages and the inconveniences before taking a sane decision whether to act or not. After proper consideration, a criminal could decide to commit or not to commit a crime depending on his choices.

---

[5] *Nguu* is a noun in the Bambili dialect and, translated into the English language, means "an ordeal." It denotes any pain inflicting process or test of honesty that may be applied to a suspect to push him/her to reveal the truth about a criminal act.

Evidently, from the classical concepts of crime emerged criminal law. Criminal law is believed to have been motivated by the sacrifice of individual liberties of citizens who sought for means of escape from war and chaotic society (Beccaria [1794] et al.). It embodied the collective concept of crime and punishment, both contributing factors to the establishment of sovereign nations (Vold 1958 and Radzinowicz 1966). This concept was opposed to the spiritualist consideration of crime as a private issue with outcomes limited solely to the victim and his family. Inasmuch as criminal law was important in deterring crimes through punishment of offenders, some of the classics (Howard [1726-90]; Bentham [1748]; Rothman et al 1995), believed that it had a major setback because it infringed seriously on people's freedoms. It placed unnecessary restrictions on individual freedoms rather than aiming at crime control and prevention. Such a restriction on individual freedoms could produce a counter-effect by increasing rather than decreasing crimes. They favored the presumption of innocence[6] as the guiding principle in administering criminal justice. They contended that punishment should be meted out proportionately to the offense without looking at the social or physical characteristics of the offender. They favored impartial laws and other crime prevention strategies rather than punishment.

Remarkably, these classical concepts of crime and punishment contributed a lot to public policies in Italy and other European nations in the eighteenth century. These ideas greatly influenced and revolutionized most state constitutions and criminal justice systems and contributed a lot to modern criminal law procedures, codes of criminal justice, the presumption of innocence during trials, human rights concerns, and law enforcement options in favor of crime control and deterrence rather than the traditional brutal order maintenance and repression that laid emphasis mostly on punishment.

Policy implications of classical criminal concept also extended to correction systems introducing the milder options of criminal treatment like reformation and rehabilitation in lieu of or in the place of imprisonment simply as punishment (Howard 1792).

Other policy implications were evident notably in France where the ancient regime operated one of the most ruthless criminal justice systems based on the presumption that the accused was guilty until he proved innocent. Unfortunately, this ugly system continues to

---

[6]   This assumption of the innocence of the accused before trial stands in stark contrast to the popularly criticized French criminal justice system that assumes that everyone accused is presumed guilty until he proves his innocence. This system, very much in practice in French-speaking Cameroon, has often been denounced for promoting the abuse of human rights. Unfortunately, the authorities have remained adamant to its practice and see no need for reform.

exist and is practiced not only in France alone but also in almost all former French colonies in Africa namely Cameroon, Cote d'ivoire, Gabon and other areas where French cultures exist.

iii. Positivist Theories

The positivist school of thought on the causality of crime that became known as modern criminology dominating the nineteenth and twentieth centuries dwelled on various biological and psychological factors to empirically prove that these were the causes of crimes. While some of the fathers of this philosophy (Lombroso [1835]) contended that biological or inborn factors of man predisposed him to criminality, others (Ferri) viewed the causes of crimes as originating from socioeconomic forces produced by political setups, notably capitalism. Other opinions (Void 1958) contended that geographical and physical forces interacting with demographic determinants—age, race, gender, religion, population, and culture—were also strongly accountable for criminality.

Disagreeing with the classical concept that explained the causes of crime as being motivated by free will and rational choice, Lombroso (b. 1835) particularly traced the causes to the biological setup of man evidenced by certain unusual physical features. Motivated by the Darwinian[7] concept that man was genetically linked to animals, a study of human anatomy and physiology of the brain (Lombroso [1909] et al.), was used to explain the causes of criminal behaviors. Biologists lay claim to two factors that essentially predispose a subject to crimes: *gender* and *environment.* For instance, they believe that criminal elements or instincts are inherent in the genetic structure of some persons and these genes are inherited by their offspring. Following an experiment carried out in Denmark in 1927 (Mednick et al.) termed cross-fostering adoption, a number of children were adopted at early ages from two different backgrounds as illustrated in the table here below.

Environment—Predisposing Factor to Crimes

---

[7] Darwin (1809-1882). Darwinism as a belief and teaching, holds that life came about as chance and has developed through an evolutionary process. He explains further that man evolved from an ape and was not created by God as taught by religion.

Table 1. ENVIRONMENT AS A PREDISPOSING FACTOR IN CRIMINAL BEHAVIOR

ORIGINAL ENVIRONMENT	Biological parents with no criminal background.	Biological parents with criminal background.
	Group A	Group B
NEW ENVIRONMENT	Adoptive parents with no criminal background	Adoptive parents with criminal background
	Group BC	Group AD
	20%	24.5%

Source: Mednick et al. (1984) (Modified)

These children with (a) biological parents with no criminal background and (b) biological parents with criminal background were raised in two different settings: (a) adoptive parents with no criminal background and (b) adoptive parents with criminal background. Then at a later stage in life, results were assessed based on their criminal or conviction records, and the following revelations were recorded: 24.5 percent of the children with criminal convictions were those from biological parents with criminal background that grew up with adoptive parents with criminal background; 20 percent were children from biological parents with criminal backgrounds that grew up with adoptive parents with no criminal background; 14.7 percent with criminal convictions were children from mental diseases (pellagra and cretinism) believed to cause mental deficiencies that predisposed people to violence and homicides. Positivist concepts assert that criminals as opposed to noncriminals could be distinguished by certain atavistic features peculiar to their biological structures. Such physiological features as sloping forehead, twisted noses, receding chins, excessive long arms, and unusual body sizes were believed to predispose subjects to criminality. Based on the characteristics mentioned above, criminals were categorized into four groups: *born criminals* (with biological structures peculiar to criminal types), *insane* (paranoiacs and alcoholics), *criminaloids* or occasional criminals, and *criminals of passion* (anger, love, or irresistible force). Body tattooing was considered a distinguishing criminal characteristic (Lombroso), though it has nowadays become fashionable. However, lacking considerable empirical support, some of the theories, notably those of Lombroso, were modified to embrace environmental variables such as climate, gender, and sociocultural organization that also claimed to predispose subjects to criminality.

b. Structural versus Differential

Structural philosophy variously viewed the origin of crime as inherent in the criminal's nature (i.e.) in his biological organization revealed through atavistic physical traits (Lombroso) that predispose him to crimes or in his psyche or mind (Freud 1920; Alexander; Healy), where the different forces (id, ego, and superego) are in perpetual conflict. When the ego has the upper hand, this victory finds a vent in external acts of criminality.

Freudian concept of crime originating from the interplay of the id, ego, and the superergo quite fairly merges with the early spiritualist view that crime originated from conflicting forces of good and evil spirits. Accordingly, biological and psychoanalytical concepts of crime contend that persons with peculiarly unusual physical features earlier mentioned above or those whose egos fail to dominate their ids become predisposed to criminality.

While structural concepts explored the causes of crime from biological and psychoanalytical perspectives, differential philosophies considered criminal causes as inherent in social disorganizations resulting from unfair sociopolitical setups (Ferri). The individualistic nature of man motivates him to set up social structures in a way to benefit him most. This concept is better explained in term of political setups. Evidently, those in position of political power usually erect social structures to favor them mostly. Hence, all forms of social controls— starting with criminal law, the criminal justice system, and associated agencies that enforce them such as the courts, the judiciary, the police, the prisons and so forth, tend to operate according to the leader's whims, often disfavoring those in the lower social order on whom these rules are applied.

Capitalist economies are often quoted as the framework on which such political setups are conceived to disfavor those at the base (Cullen, et al. 2002). The resulting unfair distribution of social and economic opportunities and services (employment, wealth, social welfare services, medical and education) breeds anger in the hearts of the disadvantaged. This situation most often escalates conflicts between the disadvantaged and those at the top of the social structure. It is this social disorganization that is believed to predispose subjects to crimes.

Differential association theories (Sutherland 1939) though partly in favor of neo-Lombrosian explanations of the causality of crime as expression of biological or psychopathological conditions, contend that the social organization of individuals has a strong motivating force on them that regulated their criminal instincts. Unfair socioeconomic and political setups usually create social stratifications that breed disorganization and animosity within the underprivileged communities. The outcome often is nonconformist lifestyles, deviant behaviors, and high crime rates. Social disorganization often weakens control that gains neighborhoods and eventually degenerates into cities and towns, implanting in its course conflicting subcultures and criminal traditions. This phenomenon tends to rival and challenge all conventional institutions. The case of Chicago that became a criminological case study (Sutherland 1939) constitutes a typical example.

These criminal cultures provide learning processes to the younger generations through constant contact or association with situational violations of social rules. Children that are used to seeing social rules or laws violated with impunity instinctively acquire this practice as a normal pattern of behavior as they grow up. Quoting the American context as an example, the differential association theory is said to explain the variation in the rate of criminality throughout the country. Juvenile delinquency and gang activities in particular, very common phenomena in the American society, may be explained variously by social disorganization, differential association, and or weakening of social control and bonding. All these ills seem to be offshoots of a system (capitalism) that institutionally favors and actively promotes an unflinching individualist pursuit of materialism (Bellah, 1991 et al).

c. Mainstream Thought

Mainstream thinking considers the causes of crime with respect to capitalist systems (e.g. America) from two perspectives: capitalism and culture. Without necessarily sanctioning on any empirical grounds the various early theories on the causes of crime, nor postulating their outright rejection in any way, mainstream school of thought in general accuses the American capitalism or market economy of being by nature criminogenic or crime prone (Lilly, Cullen, and Ball 2002).

The American-type capitalism lays more emphasis on productivity and profit making to the detriment of its tool of production (the citizens). Very little concern is paid to the well-being of the people who make the economy strong. Not only does the government fail to provide public support systems to its citizens, but it also makes it difficult for the private sector to provide these advantages to its citizens. For instance, economic institutions dominate noneconomic institutions (education, politics, and health-care) that are modeled to support the former rather than the reverse. A large segment of the population is thus pushed into deprivation. A very good case in point is President Obama's health-care bill intended to help poor Americans obtain a cheaper and government-subsidized health-care insurance. The difficulties he faced in having this bill passed in the Senate and Congress in 2011 and the derogatory label now attached to it clearly illustrate the assessment of capitalism. Even though finally passed into law, it has scarcely seen its implementation phase take off. Conservative forces in the House, in the Tea Party, and even Republican presidential candidates not only label President Obama socialist but above all have sworn to reverse and kill the bill entirely once a Republican president accedes to power.

It is no exaggeration that the American culture highly values and fosters individualism and a spirit of competitive consumerism. In order to keep pace with this spirit, the common man, who wants to respect conventional standards, overstretches himself to the point of death through numerous exhausting and lowly paid jobs. Meanwhile, those who cannot keep pace with this spirit are forced by the compelling situation to face their frustrations by employing all illegal means (drugs, violence) using lethal weapons, of which easy access to the population is more or less institutionalized. For instance, it takes as little as ten (10) minutes for a gun dealer to check and clear a potential buyer's criminal record and approve his/her purchase of any type of weapon. The unfortunate sequel of this socioeconomic imbalance is a public policy approach that favors the multiplication of correctional facilities to keep under control the ever-growing number of victims of the system (Cullen, et al.). It is worth noting that these theories impacted their respective societies and political systems where they were propounded.

Recapitulating on the early theories (e.g.) spiritualism, we learned how early people traced the genesis of crime to evil spirits/demons that took possession of individuals, pushing them to sin (crime). An individual crime or sin in those states as was believed, incurred a collective punishment from the gods to the community in several forms: earthquake, flood, plague and so forth.

In somewhat more organized and politically structured Middle Age European communities such as the Greeks, Romans, Egyptians, a more modern concept of crime started emerging. Though still viewed as a product of evil spirits, criminal effects were limited to the victim alone or his family. An individual crime seemingly did not affect the community as such. Its effect was considered to be limited just to the victim alone or to him and his family. Punishments for crimes followed public trials in institutionalized forms of battles or duels organized between the offender and the victim or family members. Of course, this put a big question mark on the fairness of criminal justice. Where the offender was the stronger person, clearly a jungle lifestyle was the rule, paying credence to the slogan "survival of the fittest." Paradoxically, crime was not only vindicated but was propagated and institutionalized. The result was a society of barbarians living a jungle lifestyle, with the more powerful preying on the weak. As time evolved, the perception of crime and justice continued to evolve positively.

The seventeenth century, characterized by its classical school of thought (some of which traced the causes of crime to the concept of free will and rational choice), ushered in a new perception of criminal justice. Seemingly dwelling more on the punitive aspect of criminal justice, the scholars of this era argued in favor of equitable punishment that should focus more on the offense rather than the offender, as well as a due process and fair trial of offenders. Evidently, these reflections inspired the conception of criminal law (Beccaria) and the criminal justice system that in turn influenced or reshaped the constitutions of most of the nations then.

The US Constitution, for instance, experienced quite a number of amendments in this light. The 1865 amendment saw the inclusion of Article XIV that was based on the *due process and equal protection of American citizens before the law* in criminal matters. Unfortunately, the French criminal justice system, borrowing from Beccaria's criminal law concept, rather instituted a hopeless system that tended to ruin instead of save its citizens. In the French criminal justice system, "Everyone accused is presumed guilty until he proves his innocence." This rather inhuman system, still in existence and practiced in France up till today, was unfortunately transplanted in French-speaking Africa through colonization. With the blessing of France, most repressive political regimes in African countries that have refused to embrace democracy fully continue to practice the system to crush it citizens. Positivist theories that view the causes of crime from biological and psychological perspectives greatly influenced policies in those nations where these concepts were propounded. The evil eugenic[8] movement of the nineteenth century, motivated by biological postulations that ascribed the causes of social problems to genetically inferior foreigners in the United States, led to the bombing in Haymarket in 1886. This concept of the origin of crime had a lot of influence on public policy formulation that so much affected the educational field, leading to the foundation of the Harvard Center where eugenics became a renowned field of studies.

i. Social Darwinism

Social Darwinism (Garofalo 1885) was another theory on crime causality that viewed society as a natural body. Hence, any violation of social laws was viewed as infringement against nature. This perception of crime created a dangerous public-policy impact within the Italian society in the nineteenth century. Drawing a comparison with the natural body, the leaders believed that all citizens had to adapt to social rules very strongly and all defaulters ought to be eliminated from the society. Those that violated social order were considered outcasts not capable of living in conventional societies (Mussolini's Italy).

Based on this concept, the criminal justice system then encouraged the violation of human rights as most offenders were eliminated physically. This concept ushered in Italy a political regime whose ideas were based on racial purity (Mussolini's authoritarian leadership) only comparable to the Nazi doctrine. Darwinist thinking compressed in the following slogans, "Struggle for survival," "Survival of the fittest," and "Let nature take its course," motivated the formulation of very conservative public policies that stood in the way of popular social programs that otherwise would have been of advantage to the lower social classes of the society. Darwinist doctrines discouraged all government-sponsored social changes or programs that directly benefited collective social strata. Such programs, in their view, only helped to perpetuate the survival of a class of lazy people that could in the long run ruin the economy of the state.

---

[8]   This is a doctrine whose roots can be traced back to Nazi Germany that believed and encouraged the selective breeding of human species with genetic characteristics judged socially desirable. The sequel, of course, was the extermination of those human species deemed socially undesirable. The Jews under Hitler's rule, of course, were victims of this system.

ii. The Strain Theory

When people are exposed to conditions of strain, they no longer respect social conventions or societal laws and rules (Merton 1957). In this condition they tend to experience a high risk of deviant behaviors (crimes). Conditions of strain are created by the absence of means or opportunities to achieve social needs. For instance, poverty (Murray 1984) and lack of jobs, educational opportunities, health services (Merton), or proper parenting (Agnew 1992) create a lot of strain on the subject. The solution to strain conditions can be provided by the state through formulation of adequate public policies that aim at equitable sharing of national resources and social benefit across the entire social strata. Unfortunately, the scope of public policy is so complicated and controversial since it touches on human aspirations. The dichotomous perception of crime causality as expressed by the various schools of thought is indicative of the difficulties policy makers normally face in getting any acceptable crime control policy appreciated by a cross section of our society. For instance, conservative opinions (social Darwinists) argue and disagree with public provision of social changes that are beneficial to the entire social strata (including the poor lower social masses) because such benefits, they believed, encouraged laziness and dependence on the state, a situation that becomes a threat to national survival.

Arguing from a moral and humanist perspective, progressive reformers favor the administration of equitable justice in trying offenders. They stand clearly against punitive justice and call for reformation and rehabilitation of the offender. This stand, of course, runs contrary to Darwinist thinking because reformative and rehabilitation programs entail national expenses that eventually can create dependence among the lower classes, statistically proven to be the most fertile breeding ground for criminals. Conservative Darwinist thinking favors social stratification because it instills a competitive spirit in individuals, thereby pushing everyone to work hard and contribute to national survival. They promote crime control policies that lay emphasis on the severity of punishment that accordingly should produce deterrent effects on criminals. They favor crime control and prevention through elimination and incapacitation.

Perceiving the criminal man as a pathetic victim of unbalanced socioeconomic structural arrangement put in place by egoistic leadership and supported and upheld by the upper class, strain theories provide an important impetus for preventive programs for juvenile delinquency as well as penal programs that favor reform and rehabilitation of the offender (Empey and Ericson 1972). The "frontier of equal opportunity," administrative action taken by late former President Kennedy, in 1960 and the founding of Mobilization for Youth (MFY) program in

New York in 1962 to fight social disorganization among the lower classes were public policies motivated by the strain theory.

Viewing capitalism as fundamentally criminogenic or causing conflicts that breed crimes, pro-Marxist thinking (Pepinsky and Quinney 1999) strongly recommends its overthrow in favor of a more peaceful moral persuasion through formal and informal negotiations, the development of social bonds, and the application of restorative instead of punitive justice as more practical approaches to solving social conflicts and crimes.

Examining the causes of crime still from another perspective, postmodernist thinking contends that the definition of crime is "a purposeful linguistic contrivance by those at the helm of the social scale as a tool of domination." Today's conflicts, they contend, result from divisive conventional institutions erected by heartless leadership to dominate and repress the poor people whom they have viciously structured to be victims of their social constructs called laws and rules (Schwartz and Friedrichs 1994). Inspiration drawn from the Chicago School of Criminology evidently suggests that public policies that promote social programs aimed at proper organization of communities and equitable distribution of social benefits go a long way to reduce delinquency and crimes (Shaw and McKay). Social programs like the Mobilization for Youth (MFY) program in New York, Cloward and Ohlin's works on *Delinquency and Opportunity*, and Empey's 1982 report on *Control and Prevention of Delinquency* were all inspired by criminology theories.

Far from being a pessimist, it is evidently clear that crime is not a virus or bacteria whose cure hopefully can one blessed day be produced in a test tube from a scientific laboratory. Secondly, man's avarice and self-centeredness will never cease to inspire a conservative stance against the good will of proponents of collective social good. In brief, the concept of equity in the distribution of public goods will continue to remain a mere abstraction as long as socioeconomic imbalances are institutionalized and nurtured. Hence, criminality is here to stay. All man needs to do is to fight to reduce the rate and its effect in society. This can be done by implementing proven research findings and recommendations in the area of crime prevention, whether they are in the form of policies affecting society or in the form of new technologies or inventions to control crime.

Western civilizations, especially the United States, in the wake of the twentieth century seem to have awakened yet to another social virus called criminality quite different from the civil strife and great economic recession following the post-World Wars era. Although a global phenomenon, criminality rates suddenly started rising at an alarming rate in this society. I am, however, in no certain way making an empirical assertion that criminality never existed before then. Far from that, what I am affirming is that the attention paid to this phenomenon in the form of research in the early twentieth century far surpassed previous efforts to examine the causes of crime. Maybe evolution in the field of technology in this century has provided man with better means of studies and research tools to pay the amount of attention witnessed recently in this field. This conclusion is made evident by the current proliferation in studies, research work, and literature in the field of criminology.

Jack Katz, Wright, Decker, and Samenow, all twentieth-century students of criminology, centered their writings on criminality and its causes in general though they approach it from different perspectives. Their major concern remains the desire to explain the causes of crime. What in man motivates him to commit crimes? This is the burning question they set out (in their writings) to find.

Jack Katz[9] examines and identifies three conditions that the criminal undergoes in the commission of a crime. Firstly, the criminal finds himself on the "path of a criminal action" (i.e. the requirements necessary for the commission of the act). Secondly, he reviews himself, how others will view him, and how to cope with external forces following the outcome—"the interpretational phase"; and thirdly, he faces the compelling forces that push the crime to completion—"the emotional process." In examining cases of cold-blooded murder of either a wife by a husband or a husband by a wife prompted, for instance, by the infidelity of one party, Katz concluded on what he termed *righteous slaughter* or the *good*[10] as the motivating force behind it.

It is doubtless that the sanctity of matrimony is a universally accepted and upheld moral value in civilized human societies. The offender in this crime of passion seemingly is defending this moral value—the sanctity of matrimony that, in other words, can be termed a sense of honor or pride. Infidelity is considered socially immoral in a matrimonial relationship. It kills the victim's honor. That is why all religions and most legislations make adultery criminal. What seems abnormal in this example is the disproportionate nature of the sanction in relation to the offense. Is it normal to punish infidelity with the loss of life? Of course, it sounds rather absurd to punish a crime with another more serious crime. This explains why offenders of such crimes, experiencing intense guilt after the commission, never attempt to cover their crimes, let alone run away from the scenes.

Katz, in *Seductions of Crime*, notes in his attempt to explain the causes of crime that every crime is characterized by special features that surround its commission and that these

---

[9]   Jack Katz; <u>Seductions of Crime</u>: "A chilling exploration of the criminal mind from juvenile delinquency to cold-blooded murder," 1988 Basic Book, US.

[10]   Katz here is referring to any universally accepted concept or what society considers an acceptable morale.

features help in the understanding of the motives behind any particular crime. Utilitarian motives would for instance, explain a violent bank robbery resulting in the loss of lives differently from an erratic school shooting by a senseless youth gang member who is simply displaying bravado in order to exhibit group prowess. Crimes motivated by utilitarian motives involve reflection and planning or "rational choice" (Katz) while those motivated by love and passion for instance, are committed on impulse. The motivating forces behind other types of crimes, whether simple shoplifting, burglary, or other forms of murder, are explained by their circumstances. In the case of a mother killing a worrisome child, seemingly the motive is to get rid of a problem by eliminating the source.

Wright and Decker,[11] while concentrating on the single crime of burglary, undertook field case studies in which they actually interrogated live burglars in the street as well as in prisons. They attempted to interpret their minds to find out what really motivates their crimes. Their findings revealed several motives in the burglars ranging from *utilitarian* (get cash), *easy living,* to get drugs, to *save a reputation,* to sustain a lifestyle. Unlike other forms of crimes that may be committed on impulse, a burglar experiences a certain amount of pressure exerted on him by utilitarian needs. In spite of the pressures, his act requires conscious planning, information gathering, and execution (rational choice).[12] **"I never go into a house where I don't know nothing about it or who's living there. You got to at least know something."** The burglar must rationalize before committing a crime in order to avoid facing the nasty sequel if caught.

Stanton Samenow[13] (clinical psychologist) takes on quite a different approach to the concept of crime causation. He contends that crime is inborn or inherent in human nature and caused by his manner of thinking. Environment does not shape someone to become a criminal. Man has a free will and can make choices. He refutes those theories that explain crime causality in terms of biological and psychophysiological structures of man, external factors such as environmental determinants, association with predisposing factors, or social disorganization. The criminal is rational, calculative, and engages deliberately in criminal acts. He may choose to commit a crime or not. Samenow strengthens his argument with the fact that criminality is the exception and not the rule in human actions. If all the above theories were true, then we would have more criminals in the society than responsible people because

---

[11] Richard Wright and Scott Decker, 1997; <u>Armed Robbers in Action:</u> Stickups and Street Culture, Northeastern Series

[12] Cullen, Ball and al; <u>Criminology Theory</u>, 2002 Sage Publications Inc. Thousand Oaks, US. Expounding on the "rational choice theory" that contends that every criminal weighs the benefits and risks of his actions before embarking on any crime.

[13] Stanton Samenow; **<u>Inside the Criminal Mind</u>**, 1984 Crown Publisher New York.

these conditions would be contagious and would affect every one of us. If poverty induced by social disorganization were to be accepted as the cause of criminal robbery, then how do we account for white-collar crimes? If genetics were a cause of crime, how do we account for the fact that in a family of five, for instance, not all the children become criminals? If it was association, then why do all prison staff not become criminals by association? In as much as there are always a few exceptions to the rule, no parent or school should be blamed for being the cause of his child or student becoming a deviant. The children or students choose to be what they are, not through the influence of parents or school environment.

Katz, Wright, and Decker (actually undertaking field research on interrogation of live criminal subjects, followed by statistical analysis to support their ideas, assertions, and conclusions or concepts on crime causation) were convinced that criminals acted on several motives: utilitarian, which involved rational choice; impulse (passion and sadism); fear of humiliation or threat to sense of pride or honor, drugs, (strain, social disorganization, or differential association theories). They are more complex in their analysis of criminal causes. They did not make generalizations but rather embarked on concrete investigations that gave them grounds to make conclusions.

As a practicing psychologist, Samenow worked with a psychiatrist, Dr. Yochelson, in a specialized unit in St. Elisabeth's Psychiatric Hospital in Washington, DC, for legally committed criminal patients. From practical diagnoses of criminal patients, interrogations, treatment, and observation, he makes a lot of generalizations. He develops his ideas and draws conclusions based solely on his experience of a rather limited number of criminal patients that he treated.

For instance, he realized that most violent crime offenders were usually wrongly decriminalized by the courts on faked insanity defenses and committed for psychiatric treatment. These offenders, he was convinced, were actually blatant liars that intelligently manipulated the magistrates and succeeded to beat the criminal justice system. Like Katz, Wright, and Decker, Samenow believes that all criminals are very calculative, egocentric, manipulative, lack empathy, and are always trying to get over the system. Most of them consciously conform to therapy in order to fake semblance of wellness and earn their way back into society where they would resume their usual criminal lifestyles. Affirming the rational choice theory, they all believe that all criminals subject themselves to proper rationalization before committing crimes.

One thing that connects these authors is, firstly, their empirical approach in the search for the causes of crimes. Secondly, they share the same convictions: the rational choice theory that affirms that criminals rationalize before committing their acts. While Samenow believes that a criminal's rationalization is influenced by free will, Katz, Wright, and Decker believe that some crimes are committed under intense emotional pressures that blind the criminal's ability to rationalize. This is the strain theory. This theory affirms that strain conditions push the criminal into the act from where he emerges with guilt and regret. Examples of such crimes are those of passion or love (rape).

PART III

ORIGIN AND CAUSES OF CRIMES

a. *Biological: Genetics*

Recent discoveries in biological sciences indicate that the more activities the human brain gets involved in right from adolescence, the more protective the subject is against the development of antisocial and criminal behaviors (Rain, Venables, and William 1995 and 1996).

- *Brain Imaging.* Most recently brain imaging, a technique used in medicine to diagnose brain disease or brain functioning, has proved that violent crime offenders have a common structural and functional deficit to the frontal and temporal lobes of the brain nearer to the ears. In conclusion, the poor functioning of these regions of the brain is believed to predispose the person to criminality.
- *Positron-Emission Tomography (PET).* In yet another technique called positron-emission tomography (PET), used to measure the metabolic activities that take place in many regions of the brains, it was revealed that prefrontal dysfunction was characteristic of murderers. This explains the reason why most murderers diagnosed with this result following a PET exam usually have their cases mitigated on grounds of insanity.

- **Cognitive Deficiencies.** Cognitive deficiencies due to reduced functioning of the angular gyrus (part of the brain) have resulted in deficiency in the reading and performance of simple arithmetic operations. This has led to educational failures and the inability to carry out occupations, often pushing the subjects to antisocial behaviors and crimes (Rain, Buchstraum, and La Casse 1997).

- **Birth Complications.** Some physical abnormalities associated with pregnancy (such as the malformation and poor development of the fetus as well as delivery complications, inadequate oxygen supply, and hypertension) have been diagnosed as affecting the development of a child's brain. Studies have shown that these conditions have often led to brain deficits that impact the individual at a later age. Such deficits, as seen in earlier studies, predispose the individual to antisocial and criminal behaviors such as *anger, aggressiveness*, and *violent outbursts*. With regards to nutrition, it was diagnosed that vitamin and mineral deficiencies such as iron, protein, and zinc greatly reduced brain functioning, resulting in antisocial and violent behaviors. Research studies conducted by Breakey (1997), Werbach (1995), and others revealed that iron deficiencies mostly affected young males, pushing them into juvenile delinquency and crimes.

- **Hormones and Castration**

Hormones. Hormones, such as male testosterone, in high levels have been found following research studies carried out by Brian (1990) and Archer (1991) to contribute very significantly in arousing aggressive and violent instincts in men and potentially predisposing them to crimes.

Whereas *castration* inversely reduces aggressive behaviors in men, low level of *cortisol*, another hormone in the body, leaves the subject under aroused, thereby developing fearlessness that in turn predisposes to criminality.

Neurotransmitters (neurons / nerve cells). Neurotransmitters are hormones that ensure information communication within the brain cells in order for the brain to perform its various functions, such as perception, sensation, eating, learning, and memory as well as the coordination of other body activities. Some of these hormones are dopamine, serotonin, norepinephrine. Research has revealed that when these hormones levels are reduced, the brain becomes deficient in its performance. This condition would predispose the subject to antisocial, violent, and criminal behaviors. Case study of people with histories of alcohol abuse, personality disorder, depression, violence, and impulsiveness revealed within their brain fluid significantly low levels of serotonin and norepinephrine.

Neurogenetics. Neurogenetics is a relatively new study on the relationship between genes and crime. These studies are actually producing positive results that indicate strong correlation between genetics and criminality. Though some of these findings are not yet conclusive, early results of some of these research studies tend to indicate that there is indeed a strong relationship between human genes and crime.

b. Environmental

Environmental. When teenagers grow up in home environments characterized by abuse or neglect and poverty or in foster homes or with criminal parents or where there is severe conflict, they develop emotional and personality deficit or what Damasio (1994) called acquired sociopathy or psychopathy. Based on a case study carried out by Rain and Stoddard in 1998 on two violent offenders, the results proved that home environment seriously impacted the violent nature of the offender. The one that grew up in a home environment with the characteristics listed above was clearly more violent than the other. This study proved that there was a strong correlation between environment and criminal predisposition.

c. Social Disorganization

Social disorganization theory[14] (Miethe et al. 1991) affirms that structural factors such as unemployment, income inequality, poverty, disrupted family ties due to broken marriages, abused and abandoned children, ethnic heterogeneity, urbanization, and rural exodus often destroy informal social ties, thereby weakening social control mechanisms. This often results in higher crime rates in the cities and, by extension, the nation. Results of extensive research carried out have often proved a strong correlation between crime rates and these indicators of

---

[14]   Developed from sociology by the Chicago School, the social disorganization theory contends that "there are ecological factors that lead to high rates of crime in these communities, and these factors linked to constantly elevated levels of "'high school dropouts, unemployment, deteriorating infrastructures, and single-parent homes'" (Gains and Miller).

social disorganization mentioned above. In fact, cities or nations with greater poverty levels, high unemployment ratios, income inequality, weak family structures, urbanization, rural exodus, and ethnic heterogeneity more likely produce higher crime rates (Land et al. 1990; Parker and Johns 2002; Sampson and Groves 1989).

A typical indicator of social disorganization considered an important predisposing factor to antisocial behavior is child abuse. It is widely believed that childhood abuse is a predisposing factor to antisocial and violent or criminal behavior. Following a case study carried out by Rain, Park and others using a medical technique called functional magnetic resonance imaging (FMRI) on the brains of violent offenders (one abused at childhood and the other not abused at all), the results indicated a positive correlation between childhood abuse and antisocial or criminal behavior. Some biological processes such as birth complications, physical abnormalities, nutrition deficiencies, and neurological defects have been found to highly correlate with antisocial or criminal behaviors. In reality, what constitutes child abuse? Instances of child abuse are abandonment; refusal to provide food, shelter, and clothing; unnecessary beatings; use of abusive language to the child; scolding; refusal to provide care and education; failure to show love; and so forth. To what extent is beating or spanking a child abusive? How can someone discipline a child without being abusive?

Disciplining a child (by a parent) lovingly with corrective intentions is clearly different from violently beating a child in anger or with harmful intentions by any person, including even the parents. This approach is very clearly affirmed by the following popular Old Testament biblical saying: **"Spare the rod and spoil the child"** (Proverbs 13:24). Incidentally, both conservative and liberal religious beliefs of the Old Testament seem to agree on this approach of child upbringing. The New Testament teachings also affirm this approach in the following chapter and lines: "The Lord disciplines those he loves, and he punishes everyone he accepts as a son. Endure hardship as discipline; God is treating you as sons. For what son is not disciplined by his father?" (Hebrews 12:6-7). By extension, teachers often refer to "the carrot and the stick approach."[15] The teacher may choose to employ either the carrot method, which involves polite and friendly encouragement/pampering the child, or the stick method, which requires some amount of discipline to dissuade the child from future

---

[15] Wikipedia: "the carrot and the stick approach." is an idiom that refers to a policy of offering a combination of rewards and punishment to induce behavior. It is named in reference to a cart driver dangling a carrot in front of a mule and holding a stick behind it. The mule would instinctively move towards the carrot because it wants the reward of food, while also moving away from the stick behind it, since it does not want the punishment of pain, thus drawing the cart along.

wrongdoings. Corrective discipline involving the use of some amount of physical beating is very commonplace in the African child-upbringing method. Is this method acceptable in the light of the biblical affirmation? Unfortunately, no statistical evidence exists to evaluate the success or failure of this method vis-à-vis the Western approach that entirely eschews physical correction of any sort in preference to the carrot method. In some Western cultures, child protection laws are so strict that they sometime tend to be counterproductive in child upbringing, thereby defeating the very purpose of their formulation in the first place. For instance, reported cases of child abuse in the US often result in the child being removed from the parent(s) by Child Protective Services and placed in foster care until the child becomes an adult (about 21 years old). The consequence of this long separation is that, a condition of estrangement is created between the abused child and the parent (s). When this happens, the child starts manifesting anti-social behaviors like delinquency; disobedience, refusal to attend school, and involvement in drugs and gangs. We realise in the long run that the very good intention of protecting the society has been compromised by policies that are too strictly enforced. The time of separation in foster care is too long. A shorter period in foster care and frequent but surpervised short stay with the parents could remedy the situation.

d. Politico-Economic

How does politics affect the crime rate of a nation? Democratic systems guarantee popular consultations that result in the expression of the people's will through elections. Constitutions and leaders that ensue from fair electoral processes most often adopt federal systems or some popularly acceptable form of power-sharing arrangement or decentralization of power and administration that guarantee independent legislature and judiciary. These structures in a democratic system ensure the rule of law and justice, thereby safeguarding and guaranteeing popular aspirations such as minority interest, merit-based distribution of training and employment opportunities, equitable sharing of national wealth, social services (education and health), economic opportunities, and developmental infrastructures. In political systems where leaders ensue from populist (democratic) consultations and elections, their jobs and positions depend on voters' continued support. As such, they are compelled to work with the people to formulate or develop policies that address their voters' concerns. Meanwhile, local political leaders and administrators that earn their jobs and positions through appointment from higher political leaders who accede to power through undemocratic processes always govern their people with arrogance and disrespect because they feel insulated from these people by those that appoint them. As such, the people have little or no say and cannot influence public policies. Good examples can be drawn from city governments. Mayors, city councilors, and administrators that are appointed by decrees and not elected by popular votes often feel insulated from group demands (Wilson and Boland, 1978). Since such appointments are often based on favoritism and not merit or professional expertise, inefficiency and poor output result from this, creating social deviants and criminals. Using the example of the police and city crime, these authorities often pay little regard to citizens' demands for more crime control and prevention policies as they do not depend on these voters for their continued job tenure. Unfortunately, these citizens have little or no leverage over the decisions of these managers. They cannot influence policing style and crime policies (Feiock 2004; Jeong and Kim 2003; Sharp 2002). This situation leads to negative police-community relations, and the result is higher crime rates (Jacobs and Carmichael 2002). Drawing from neo-Marxist research by O'Connor (1973), Thomas D. Stucky affirms in his political resource theory that "elite interests predominantly shape welfare state policies and that welfare state programs do little to alleviate inequality. Pluralist formations stress the role of partisan politics in shaping welfare policies." The unfortunate result of this is the creation of social disorganization that in turn promotes increased crime rates in the society. In another vein, the type of political system operated and the manner in which a national territory is organized for administrative purposes have an effect on its overall crime rate. History is there for us to revisit and see how monarchies and totalitarian, autocratic, and dictatorial forms of government always created social disorganization, thereby breeding crimes, unrest, and dysfunctional societies that often result in popular revolutions and total social collapse. All human beings irrespective of their cultures, languages, race, and so forth aspire for freedom (of association and speech), equality in economic opportunities, and peaceful cohabitation. When politicians do not balance these equations through popular consultations but instead use decrees to break up natural, cultural, and linguistic groupings and band people together against their wishes, they invariably breed the germ of evil and criminality in the peoples' minds. When through greed they monopolize political power and think that they can lord it all over millions of citizens, the germ of criminality is bred in the minds of those sections of the population left out in political cold. When politicians are partisan in the exploitation and management of national wealth, share employment inequitably, distribute social services and other development infrastructure discriminatorily, they are indeed seeding discontent that may eventually breed antisocial behaviors and crimes.

PART IV

A. CATEGORIES AND TYPES OF CRIMES

i. Treason, Felony, and Misdemeanors

Criminal law categorizes crime into three main categories, namely, treason, felony, and misdemeanors.

Treason is the highest category of crimes. It is a crime that affects the sovereignty of a state or nation. For instance, waging war against a nation, assassinating a president, or conspiring with or collaborating with the enemies to attack a nation is engaging in a treasonable offense. Most often the commission of this offense if not well handled may result in war—civil war or war between nations. The example of the Rwandan civil war in 1994 is a case in point. The two Rwandan tribes—minority Tutsis and majority Hutus—slaughtered each other in a civil war that has become known as the Rwanda Genocide.[16] This war was sparked by the death of their president in a plane crash, which the minority Tutsis that controlled political power alleged was caused by the Hutus.

A *felony* is a serious crime that is normally punishable with a sentence of more than one year of imprisonment and some monetary fines depending on the code of criminal procedure

---

[16]   In 1994 the presidents of Rwanda and Burundi (Mr.Juvénal Habyarimana and Cyprien Ntaryamira, respectively), neighboring East African nations, were killed in a plane crash in Rwanda. This incident ignited a civil war resulting in the slaughter of majority Hutus by the minority Tutsi that controlled political power in Rwanda. The effect of this war spilled over into the Democratic Republic of Congo and continues to drag on till today.

of the nation in question. Examples of felonies include violent crimes (murder, aggravated assault, arson, rape or sexual offenses, burglary, smuggling, and sale of outlawed drugs).

A *misdemeanor* is a less serious crime punishable with a sentence of less than one year of imprisonment and some monetary fines as determined by code of criminal procedure of every nation concerned. Examples are traffic offenses (speeding above posted speed limits, violation of stop signs, simple assault, drunk driving, public soliciting, and panhandling).

ii. Common Crimes or Offenses

Statistically, common offenses can be grouped into three categories: *property crimes*, *violent crimes*, and the *use of illegal drugs* (marijuana, cocaine, narcotics, and amphetamines).

- **Property Crimes**

Property crimes are crimes such as theft and willful destruction or damage of property belonging to others, government, or private property. Examples of property crimes are the following:

❖ **Vandalism:** This is willful destruction or damage of another person's property without his/her permission. It includes destruction, defacement, disfiguration caused by tearing, cutting, breaking, marking and painting, drawing, and covering with filth or any action as prohibited by the law.

❖ **Larceny/Theft:** This is the act of unlawfully taking, carrying, or leading away another person's property (e.g. shoplifting, pocket picking, purse snatching, or stealing from someone's car).

❖ **Burglary:** This is unlawful entry into a structure (building) to commit a felony or any other crime. It is usually carried out stealthily or cautiously by the offender when certain that there is no person present to witness the crime. Burglars usually enter into a facility by force, opening a door or window. There are three types of burglars:

  ➢ Amateur
  ➢ Juvenile
  ➢ Professional

Amateur and juvenile burglars would walk around or go far looking for the opportunity to steal. They may also steal on the spur of the moment as the opportunity presents itself. They often look as they loiter around for targets that are easily accessible with very little chances of detection.

Professional burglars usually prepare and execute a well-planned crime after conducting a thorough surveillance of their target area. Important clues that officers on patrol should not miss are strangers loitering aimlessly around homes or neighborhoods where they do not live. Officers should stop and question such suspects. Such preemptive actions may help deter potential burglaries. Officers responding to burglary calls should always be alert and extremely cautious because burglars are usually nervous and panicky and can be very harmful. Most burglars always carry weapons and are ready to use them when taken by surprise.

- ❖ **Arson:** This is a willful or malicious burning or an attempt to burn down a dwelling place or house, public building or edifice, motor vehicle, aircraft, ship, or any other property of another person. Arson may be committed with or without the intention to steal or defraud or to conceal evidence. It is considered criminal when the element of intent is clearly established. Arson resulting from suspicious or unknown sources or accident cannot be classified as criminal. It is often difficult to determine whether an act of arson is criminal or not because evidence used in committing the act is usually destroyed by the fire. Criminal investigators should always be very careful when making any determination about acts of arson. They should search very keenly for clues on the scene that might help them to draw any firm conclusion. Arson may be committed for the following reasons: to cover up another crime, for economic gains, to take revenge for a perceived wrong done to the arsonist, or to vent pent-up political grievances.

iii. Violent Crimes

- ❖ **Assault.** It is an unlawful attack on a person by another. Assaults are not premeditated. They occur on the spur of the moment, following acts of provocation or emotional encounters. Verbal threats do not constitute assault.
- ❖ **Simple Assault.** This type of assault is carried out without the intent to cause serious bodily harm or mortal injury to the victim. Simple assaults do not involve the use of any sort of weapon.

- ❖ **Aggravated Assault.** This is an unlawful serious attack on a person by another with the intention of inflicting severe or bodily injury on the person. It usually involves the use of a weapon or some object that may likely kill the person or cause great bodily harm. Once weapons like firearms, knives, or other dangerous weapons are involved, it is not necessary for the victim to have been inflicted with wounds for the act to be classified as aggravated assault. This is so because it certainly would be so had the crime been completed; that is, there is nothing like an attempted aggravated assault. There is no mitigation to aggravated assault.
- ❖ **Robbery.** It is the act of taking away or attempting to take anything valuable from someone's care, custody, or control by use of force or threat of force or violence thereby subjecting the victim to a state of fear.
- ❖ **Armed Robbery.** This is when the act of robbery involves the use of weapons. Most robbers are always armed and ready to use the weapons if need arises. In general, robbery involves confronting another person. As such, the chances of being noticed by a third party or other people are high. Consequently, investigators may easily get evidence of robbery from observers of the act. Professional robbers usually plan their crimes with the assistance of accomplices who serve as informants gathering information about their targets and passing it to them. Statistics reveal that many officers have been wounded or killed by armed robbers.

iv. White-Collar Crimes

White-collar criminality can tersely be defined as the crime of the upper social class. It is widely carried out by upper-class men of the political, business, and professional world. Edward Ross[17] in *White-Collar Criminal* calls them criminaloids and goes further to define them as those people **"who by flagitious practices have not yet come under the effective barn of the public opinion. Often, indeed, they are guilty in the eyes of the law; but since they are not culpable in the eyes of the public and in their own eyes, their spiritual attitude is not that of the criminal."** White-collar crimes are committed through embezzlement and misappropriation of public funds; misrepresentation in financial statements of corporations, in advertising, and salesmanship; duplicity in the manipulation of power;

---

[17] Gilbert Geis, 1968, <u>White Collar Criminal: The offender in Business and the professions</u>, Atherton, New York. Pages 25-26

fraudulent practices in taxation, billing, and commercial bribery; misapplication of short weights and measures; and low grading of commodities to name just these few. In order to make our understanding of white-collar crimes very simple and clear, we will examine the Medicaid sector and see how this crime can be committed or is very easily committed in there.

Our concern here is to determine whether Medicaid fraud falls within the definition of white-collar criminality. Firstly, what is Medicaid? Medicaid is a special fund allocated by government to cover the cost of medical care for poor and elderly people in the society. In Medicaid, white-collar crimes can be committed in the following ways: performing of unnecessary medical diagnostics to patients and billing them to Medicaid fund. To be more explicit, a physician that orders an EKG examination for a patient (who consults his services for a simple cold) in order to get paid by Medicaid, whereas he could have given him a simple treatment for cold, is guilty of white-collar crime. It could also be in the form of billing for services not rendered, receiving kickbacks, deliberately duplicating bills, or falsely making wrong entries on cost reports—all these are white-collar crimes.

Like every crime, there is always a perpetrator and a victim. The poor people for whom Medicaid funds are allocated and the government that provides the funds to pay the medical services of these people are the victims of Medicaid fraud. While the poor people are underserved or subjected to unnecessary medical services, the government is made to overpay money for services that the people do not really need or for services not really rendered.

The main actors or perpetrators of Medicaid fraud are those professionals in the medical or health chain, starting with the physician who initiates the process, through the laboratories and other health practitioners that play a part in the treatment of patients: gynecologist, dentist, ophthalmologist, pharmacist, ambulance service, private medical transport services, hospitals, and private clinics (called Medicaid Mills in California).

The context of Medicaid fraud is so vast but commences with the physician's office where unnecessary diagnoses are initiated, private clinics ("Medicaid Mills"), and billing departments of the services concerned. At the level of regulatory boards, we have "Medicaid Fraud Control Units (MFCU)" that fail to enforce certain regulations found violated, or at the level of even states that failed to create MFCU; at the level of investigations and prosecution, state attorneys' offices where certain fraudulent acts may be covered up in exchange for bribes; or at the level of the Congress or Senate where lobbyists may influence policies to defend or protect a favored business or professional association's interest. It may even be at the level of the treasury departments where some authorities may knowingly authorize the payment of fraudulent bills in exchange for some kickbacks.

Accordingly, preventing Medicaid fraud means ensuring physicians' practices are honest and clean. This implies scrupulously investigating, detecting, and punishing fraudulent practices of physicians. But this is not always easy because of a number of legal and structural impediments placed on the investigator's path. For instance, an investigator's effort is limited by the legally imposed respect of privacy law, restricted access to information about physicians' practices and patients' medical records, reluctance of prosecution or courts to pronounce severe or prison sentences on guilty physicians because of their important social status. Most often the practice is either to devalue their offenses as less important or to impose professional sanctions that end in mere suspension of Medicaid services.

Government needs to slacken the tight strings on privacy laws and let investigators more ease to penetrate into the practices of those that deal with Medicaid so as to uncover these fraudulent practices. The courts, on the other hand, should mete out equitable sanctions to fraudulent practitioners irrespective of social status because their crimes affect a greater population of the society than burglary, which affects a single person for which the accused is punished severely with imprisonment. Everyone should be treated equally before the law as enshrined in the supreme law of the state. The outcome is that the poor people continue to be deprived of proper medical care as Medicaid funds are swindled into physicians' and associated groups' pockets. The apprehension that physicians may withdraw participation in this national health plan through Medicaid if stringent sanctions were imposed on them can be challenged by the growing numbers of doctors in the United States. The perpetrators in this particular case deserve proportionate imprisonment terms. Their acts affect by far a larger portion of the community than that of an isolated thief.

v. Cyber-Crimes

Cyber-crimes are those crimes that involve the use of the computer and network systems. They are fairly new and started surfacing with the development of the computer networking and the Internet technologies in 1958 in the US. Some examples are the following:

Phishing. This is the act of sending out fake e-mails to Internet users, posing as if they are from legitimate organizations like financial institutions (banks, credit unions, and so forth) with the intention to obtain confidential and financial information. Such e-mails usually contain fake websites that replicate the real ones.

Hacking. This is the act of sending out small computer programs called malware or malicious software that exploit weaknesses in the operating systems. They often appear in the victim's computer in the form of pop-ups. Once the victims ignorantly downloads and installs them, they spread viruses that destroy the computer, or they enable the hacker to gain access and take over control of the victim's Internet activities and exploit it to achieve his intended goal.

Bot Attacks. This is a process whereby someone using a bot code penetrates into other computers, turns them into zombies, steals information, and uses it to spread viruses that destroy other computers and network systems.

Scamming. This is currently the most widely spread crime. It is the act of deceiving and extorting money or some other financial/material gains from someone through false promises. Internet scammers do send out checks to individuals, requesting the victims to cash them and send the money back to them in anticipation of some bigger amounts to be dished out to the victim. Sometimes they may request banking information from their target with promises to transfer or deposit funds into the bank account so they can share with the victim. Once in possession of this information, they can easily hack into the victim's account and carry out dangerous banking transactions like money transfers from the victim's account to their benefit. See below sample scam check and letters.

It consists of a letter with clear instructions on what to do and a genuine bank check addressed to the author of this book. Fortunately, he never fell to it.

Fig. 1. SAMPLE OF SCAM BANK CHECK

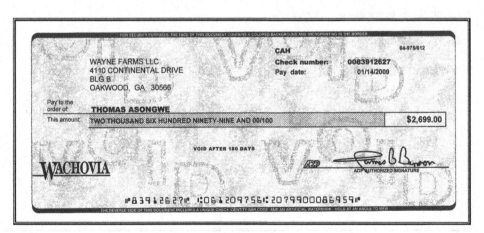

(Source: Author's Research Records)

Fig. 2. SAMPLE OF SCAM LETTER

MERIT GRANT INC.

ATTN:
THOMAS ASONGWE
9311 WILLOW POND LN
BURKE VA 22015

SERIAL NO: IMC/ 04-J-N-09.

On behalf of **The Grants Association,** we are proud to announce that your grant in the amount of **$50,000.00 (Fifty thousand dollars/00)** has been approved.

As soon as your Federal and International Administration Fee of ($2,699.00) has been paid with the Attached Check and our Commission of ($5,000.00) deducted from your grant, a certified check in the amount of ($45,000.00) will be forwarded to your mailing address.
Please contact us at **1-514-625-3962** immediately and one of our agents will verify your file with you to prevent any delay of the release of your grant to you.

Your approved documentation was sent to our company **The Grant Board of Commission from the processing office.** Everything was evaluated by our legal department and this leaves you the sole beneficiary of this grant.
This grant is not a loan to you. It can be used to start a small business, pay tuition fees, make a down payment on a home, do housing repairs or pay for medical expenses.
Once your payment is confirmed, and the deduction of our Commission Fee is made, you will be receiving your balance within 2 business days through DHL, FEDEX or UPS services.

All grants should be claimed by Feb 09, 2008.

Thank you and congratulations from all of us at **Merit Grant Inc.**

Sincerely

Kenny Maxwell.

Correspondent Agent.

8043 15th Ave W, Vancouver, Bc, V1y 6n6, Tel: 1-514-625-3962.

Source: Author's Research Records)

Fig 3: SAMPLE SCAM LETTER SOLICITING BANKING INFORMATION

From: Elham Abunura <elhamabu23@gmail.com>;
To: <>;
Subject: HELLO & Greetings to you.
Sent: Mon, Oct 7, 2013 9:38:28 AM

HELLO & Greetings to you.

I am writing this letter in confidence believing that if it is the wish of God for you to help me and my family, God almighty will bless and reward you abundantly and you would never re-great this.

I am a female student from Burkina Faso University Teachings Hospitals (BUTH) Burkina Faso, Ouagadougou. My father died earlier eight months ago and left me and my junior brother behind. He was a king, which our town citizens titled him over sixteen years ago before his death. I was a princess to him and my mother is not literate enough to know my father's entire wealth.

He left the sum of USD $4.350.000.00US dollars. In a security company, this money was annually paid into my late fathers account from the Gold mining company and Colton processing Company operating in our locality for the compensation of youth and community development in our jurisdiction.

I don't know somewhere in abroad to invest the money so that my father's kindred will not take over what belongs to my father and our family because I'm a female according to our African tradition.

Now, I urgently need your humble assistance to move this money from the security company to your bank account that is why I felt happy when I saw your contact because o strongly believe that by the grace of God, you will help me invest this money wisely. I am ready to pay 20% of the total amount to you if you can help us in this transaction and another 10% interest of annual after Income to you, for handling this transaction for us, which you will strongly have absolute control over. If you can handle this project sincerely and also willing to assist me in lifting this money to your country, kindly reach me.

Please, note that this transaction is 100% risk free and I hope to start the transaction as quick as possible, I will send you my photograph as soon as I hear from you.
Yours sincerely,
Princess. Elham Abunura

Source: Author's Research Records)

vi. Hate Crimes

The law recognizes hate crime as a category of crimes motivated by bias. It usually occurs when a perpetrator attacks a victim because of differences in religious beliefs, race, disability, ethnicity, nationality, age, gender, social status, political affiliation, and sexual orientation. It is manifested in the form of physical assault, injury, property damage, bullying, harassment, verbal abuses, insults, and even murder. The most recent example that took place in the month of March 2012 in Florida, United States, was the shooting to death of a harmless young black boy of seventeen years by a neighborhood watchman called Zimmerman. Some groups or individual perpetrators even manifest this crime by printing offensive graffiti around the premises or on the cars of their victims. During and after World War I, the Nazis perpetrated hate crimes against the Jews. In the 1980s in America, groups like the Ku Klux Klan (KKK) and skinheads perpetrated a lot of hate crimes against blacks. In South Africa during the apartheid era, a lot of hate crimes were perpetrated by both whites and blacks against each other. In Cameroon, law enforcement officers, most of them French speakers, profile and discriminate against some English speakers because of their hatred of the English language with which they are uncomfortable.

vii. Civil Rights Crime

These are crimes that were committed mostly against the black people of America during the civil rights movements in the '60s. The Birmingham, Alabama, Baptist Church bombing on September 15, 1963, that resulted in the killing of four black girls is an example of civil rights crimes. There were isolated or individually sponsored as well as collective or organized crimes, like those committed by the KKK against black Americans or by the Nazis against Jews in Germany. Some were committed by uniformed officers sponsored by governments or on individual basis. In most cases, the perpetrators (law enforcement officers) were never punished for these offenses. The following photo illustrates police brutality during the black civil rights movement in the '60s.

Fig. 4. CIVIL RIGHTS MOVEMENT—POLICE BRUTALITY ON PROTESTERS

(Source: Wikipedia)

viii. Racially Motivated Crimes

Racially motivated crimes are those that stem from hatred of one race by a person or group of persons from a different race. Racially motivated crimes continue to prevail in all heterogeneous societies where people with different racial, linguistic, religious, and cultural backgrounds are bound to cohabit. For instance, whites, blacks, Asians, Arabs, Christians, Muslims, and so forth. After the Second World War, the KKK (a white supremacist group) reemerged in America. It strongly countered the Civil Rights Movement with a lot of racially motivated crimes. In self-defense, the blacks formed the Black Panther Party. Both groups got involved in racially motivated crimes that caused so much social unrest and violence resulting in a lot of human casualties. The photo below illustrates some of the violence committed against blacks in the '60s by the KKK.

FIG. 5. BIRMINGHAM CHURCH BOMBING, 1963, ALABAMA, USA

(Source: Wikipedia)

ix. Human Trafficking / Involuntary Servitude, Slavery, and Prostitution

The best definition of human trafficking seems to be that contained in *The United Nations Protocol to Prevent, Suppress and Punish Trafficking in Persons, especially Women and Children*. Also known as the Palermo Protocol established in 2002, it defines human trafficking as follows:

> **"Trafficking in persons shall mean the recruitment, transportation, transfer, harboring or receipt of persons, by means of the threat or use of force or other forms of coercion, of abduction, of fraud, of deception, of the abuse of power or of a position of vulnerability or of the giving or receiving of payments or benefits to achieve the consent of a person having control over another person, for the purpose of exploitation. Exploitation shall include, at a minimum, the exploitation or the prostitution of others or other forms of sexual exploitation, forced labor or services, slavery or practices similar to slavery, servitude or the removal of organs."**

Human trafficking is thus the act of illegally and through the use of force abducting or recruiting and transferring or transporting people against their will to other regions or countries and subjecting them to forced labor with the intent to exploit them for personal gains. The easiest and greatest numbers of victims of human trafficking are women and children. The trend of movement is mostly from underdeveloped to more developed countries. Exploitation of victims is performed in various forms ranging from forceful and non-remunerated work, slavery, and prostitution. The men and children are used to serve as domestic servants in private homes or hotels and restaurants or in industries on very little or no salaries while the women and young girls are used as prostitutes in brothels while their owners receive payment for their services. Citizens of countries that are economically poor or are mismanaged through corruption or dictatorship are easy preys to human trafficking. The bar chart below indicates human-trafficking percentage distribution based on gender and the kind of exploitation to which the victims are subjected.

Table 2. HUMAN TRAFFICKING STATISTICS

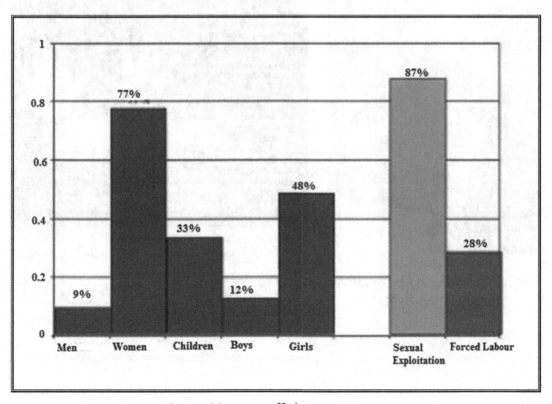

Source: Humantraffickingstatistic.net

International Labor Organization (ILO) statistics state that at least 12.3 million people are currently victims of human trafficking. Majority of them are women and girls. Children who account for approximately 20 percent of all trafficked persons constitute the greatest casualties of this nasty trade. Further still, 1.8 million children are exploited every year, according to ILO statistics, by the commercial sex industry. The Internet is full of websites created and run by con men that deceive and trap their prey with promises of legitimate jobs abroad. This explains why in underdeveloped countries it is not uncommon to find long lines of young men and women struggling to obtain visas to go abroad for work. Those that usually succeed to obtain entry visas are often embarrassed to find themselves on arrival in the host countries in sweatshops or brothels where they are forced to work hard in order to pay off huge debts to their traffickers.

Fig. 5. GIRL ENTRAPPED IN SEX SLAVERY

Fig. 6. HOMELAND SECURITY BLUE CAMPAIGN AGAINST HUMAN TRAFFICKING

(Source: International Organization for Migration-IOM)

(Source: ICE-Home Land Security)

Fig. 7 YOUNG GIRLS ENTRAPPED IN SEX SLAVERY IN ASIA

(Source: Redressonline)

Fig. 8 GLOBAL TRAFFICKING OF WOMEN, CHILDREN, AND MEN

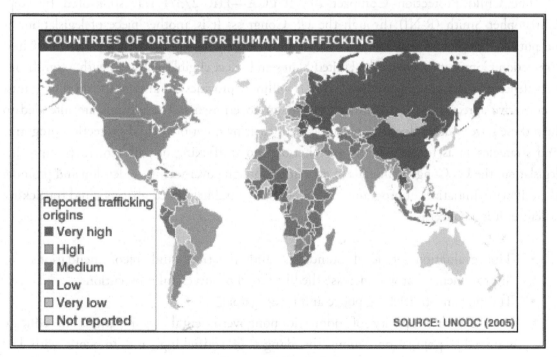

(Source: Wikipedia)

In spite of the effort deployed by most governments as well as human rights organizations to combat human trafficking, these predators always easily find their way through, thanks to their highly corrupting abilities and some vulnerable and heartless law enforcement agents in some countries that readily give in to their corruption. While counting on the effort of governments and private organizations that fight hard to stop this evil practice, law enforcement agents are strongly requested to stand up to their professional standards and commitment and honestly enforce anti-trafficking legislations in their respective countries. It is in this light that the Trafficking Victims Protection Act (TVPA) and Child Protection Compact Act (CPCA—HR 2737) were passed by the US Congress. The TVPA defines human trafficking as follows:

a. sex trafficking in which a commercial sex act is induced by force, fraud, or coercion, or in which the person induced to perform such an act has not attained 18 years of age; or
b. the recruitment, harboring, transportation, provision, or obtaining of a person for labor or services, through the use of force, fraud, or coercion for the purpose of subjection to involuntary servitude, peonage, debt bondage, or slavery.

The Child Protection Compact Act (CPCA—HR 2737) was sponsored by Rep. Christopher Smith (R-NJ) through the US Congress. It is another piece of legislation, as he puts it, "to protect and rescue children from trafficking by the establishment of Child Protection Compacts between the United States and select eligible countries with a significant prevalence of trafficking in children." CPCA willingly provides funding in the form of grants, cooperative agreements, and contracts to foreign governments. These funds are intended to help these governments develop and implement their own national child protection programs and strategies so as to combat the exploitation and trafficking of children. In passing this legislation, the US Congress intends to encourage foreign governments to develop and promote the following initiatives or programs that hopefully should help in combating child trafficking wherever it is a concern.

• The evaluation of legal standards and practices and recommendations for improvements that will increase the likelihood of successful prosecutions.
• Training anti-trafficking police and investigators.
• Building the capacity of domestic nongovernmental organizations to educate vulnerable populations about the danger of trafficking, and to work with law enforcement to identify and rescue victims.

- Creation of victim-friendly courts.
- Development of appropriate after-care facilities for rescued victims.
- Development and maintenance of data collection systems.
- Development of regional cooperative plans with neighboring countries to prevent cross-border trafficking of children and child sex tourism.

Fig. 9, Pie chart statistics on human trafficking

(Source: Wikipedia)

x. Organized Crimes (Gangs)

The term *gang* is so varied and difficult to affix to a universally accepted definition. However, the US Department of Justice and Homeland Security define it as **"an association of three or more individuals that adopt a commonly agreed identity and a common name, slogan, identifying sign, symbol, tattoo or physical mark, style or color of clothing, hair style or hand sign or graffiti that they use to create an atmosphere of fear and intimidation in their communities."** There are youth and adult gangs. They often engage in violent crimes to show their power and to preserve their group's reputation or to gain economic resources.

Organized crimes are illegal activities carried out by members of very highly structured and centralized network of criminals or gangs with the primary purpose of making monetary profits, creating some notoriety, or achieving some political goals. They may be transnational, national, or locally based, such as street gangs. They often engage in gun violence, human trafficking, and intellectual property theft. For example, the famous Latin American drug cartels, the Sicilian Mafia (Cosa Nostra), the Mara Salvatrucha or Salvadorian MS-13, the Italian American Mafia, and the Serbian Mafia are examples of criminal organizations that carry out organized crimes. The notorious Al-Qaeda is a terrorist organization that engages in politically motivated crimes.

xi. Environmental Crimes

Environmental crimes are illegal activities or acts committed by an individual, corporate entity, or government department that affect individual and public safety or the safety of another state or country. The following are examples of environmental crimes:

- The careless use of pesticides endangering individual or public safety
- The illegal disposal of hazardous waste that pose all sorts of risks to people
- The exportation of hazardous material or waste without the permission of the receiving country
- The illegal discharge of pollutants to a water source
- The removal and inappropriate disposal of regulated asbestos containing material not consistent with the country's laws and regulations
- The illegal importation of certain restricted or regulated chemicals into the country
- Dangerous tampering with drinking water, natural gas, or petrol supply sources or lines

B. CRIME ANALYSIS

i. Definition

Crime analysis is a law enforcement function that makes use of a set of techniques and computer software in the study of crimes. It involves a systematic exploration of crime-related data to identify and examine patterns and trends in crimes and disorders within a geographic region (e.g. part of a city, city, town, region, or country) in order to draw significant conclusions that may help improve law enforcement crime control and prevention operations and strategies or policy formulation and the administration of criminal justice.

ii. Purpose

After identifying and examining crime data and reports, analysts would be able to draw informed conclusions based on crime patterns and trends that would be used for the following purposes by the departments concerned with such functions, namely, investigators, prosecutors, judges and management:

- To solve crimes
- In developing effective strategies and tactics to prevent future crimes
- To find and apprehend offenders
- To prosecute and convict offenders
- To improve public safety and quality of life
- To enhance internal law enforcement operations
- To prioritize patrol and investigation
- To detect and solve community problems
- To plan future departmental budget and resource needs
- To enact effective crime control and prevention policies
- To educate and solicit public cooperation in crime prevention and control programs and strategies

iii. Method

Crime analysis is quite tedious and time demanding. It can be performed at all levels, including tactical, operational, strategic, and management levels of the police. The analyst plows daily through enormous piles of crime reports from investigations, arrests, traffic, phone communications, calls for service, public complaints, and so forth. Using any of the following computer analytical software applications: IBM SPSS Crime Analytic solutions (CPAS), Police Computer Aided Dispatch Systems (CAD), Hyperion Essbase, Integeo Map intelligence systems, and so forth (see fig 10. below), he can track statistics and perform data analysis and enquiries, crime mappings, and so forth. He studies and analyzes police beats and work-shift configurations and proposes recommendations to hierarchy for improvement in areas where there are lapses. He prepares information for public safety and for courtroom presentation during trials. He also answers questions from the public through the press and provides information to support police operations. Using Hyperion designer 207 application (see fig. 10), the analyst can operate crime filtering based on crime type, day of the week when it occurred, and status of the criminal (whether the criminal was apprehended, ignored, or still at large). This process would enable police management to plan and improve on law enforcement strategies and operations based on crime trends revealed by the analysis. For instance, if a certain crime type is recurrent in a unique location on a particular day of the week or month of the year, police policy makers may draw certain conclusions based on this crime characteristic. They would try to understand what factors were available on this location and day of the week that favored this crime type. This information would help them decide to place the area under increased surveillance, by mobilizing more patrols officers on the spot or deploying other crime prevention or deterrent strategies to control this crime type. Depending on the severity of the crime, policy makers may even recommend the creation of police precincts in the area in order to ensure permanent presence.

Fig.10 SAMPLE CRIME FILTERING SCREEN

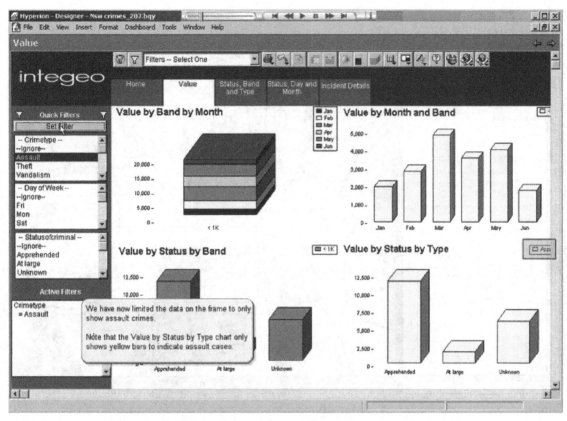

(Source: dashboadspy.wordpress.com with: Integeo pty Ltd)

Fig. 11 SAMPLE CRIME ANALYSIS DASHBOARD MAPPING

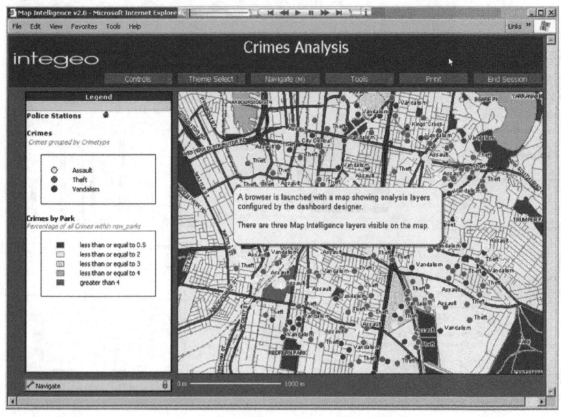

(Source: Integeo pty Ltd)

Fig. 12 SAMPLE CRIME FILTERING BY LOCATION AND TYPE

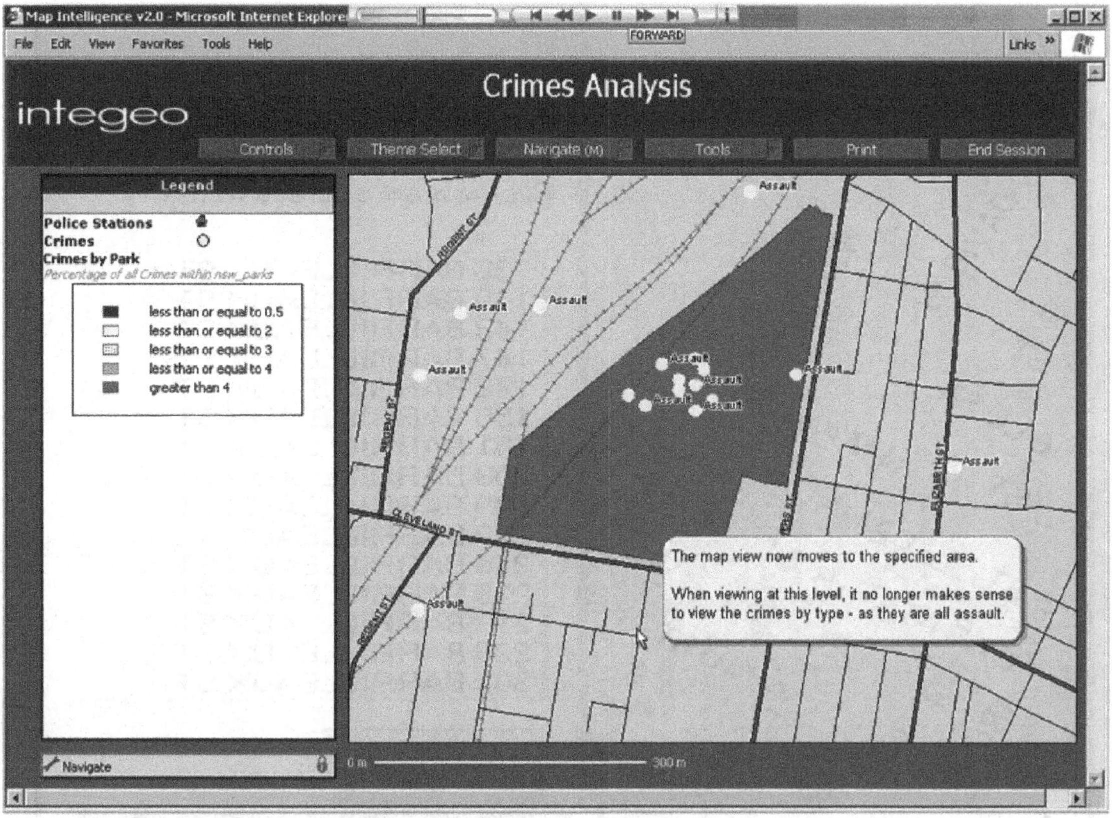

(Source: Integeo pty Ltd)

Below is a sample mapping of a crime location using ledsMapping Integrated Mapping Software application by Zuercher Technologies. On an active computer screen, the dispatcher can click on any of the addresses on the "Review Search Results" expanded window (fig. 13) to map the address in the application and the location of a crime, and the shortest route (fig. 14) to that location within the city will be displayed. This helps the dispatcher to assign a police officer located nearest to this location to rush to the scene immediately for intervention. It also helps to keep the dispatcher constantly abreast with the unfolding of events on the crime scene.

Fig. 13 SAMPLE MAPPING OF A CRIME LOCATION

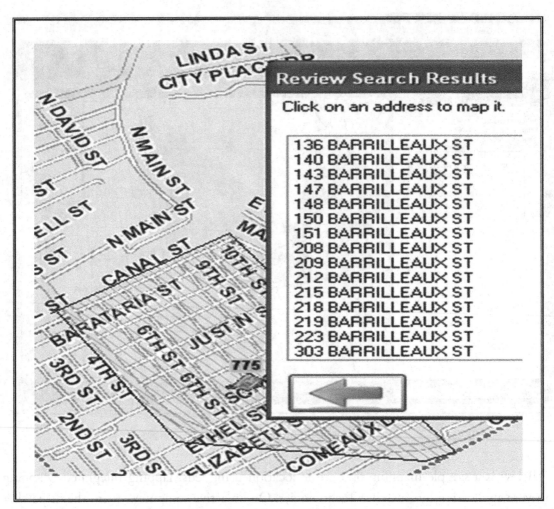

(Courtesy: zuerchertechnologies)

Fig. 14 SAMPLE MAPPING INDICATING A SHORT
ROUTE TO A CRIME LOCATION

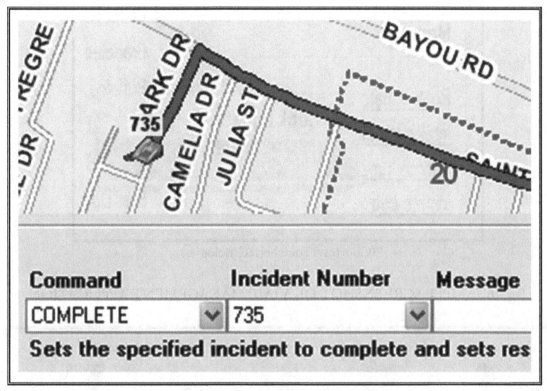

(Courtesy: zuerchertechnologies)

Ledsjail Jail Management Systems (JMS) by Zuercher Technologies also provides computer solutions to jails and corrections departments for booking and management of convict records. Figures 15 and 16 are sample screenshots of jail management software systems Ledsjail (JMS).

Fig. 15 SAMPLE SCREENSHOT OF A JAIL MANAGEMENT APPLICATION

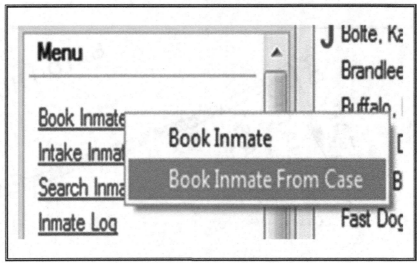

(Courtesy: zuerchertechnologies)

Fig. 16 SAMPLE SCREENSHOT OF A JAIL MANAGEMENT APPLICATION

(Courtesy: zuerchertechnologies)

"Some other computer software applications that equally provide easy solutions to Law enforcement, Jails and Corrections management are Lock&track Corrections information system by Locktrack LLC and Code3 jail management systems by Delphi Enterprise. Thanks to their use of standard windows commands and conventions such as toolbars, title-bar buttons and drop down menus, they provides ease of use for the staff and administrators. These applications enable instant data entry and access to inmate information such as admission or incarceration, offender information, court trial appointments, release, post-release activities and reporting. Lock&track system is much appreciated because it can be run on stand alone desktop computers as well as on small network of office computers. See sample screenshots of lock&track system in fig:17 and fig: 18 below" and code3 detention management system in Fig 19 below.

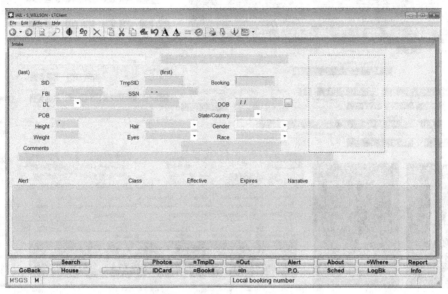

(Source: Locktrack)

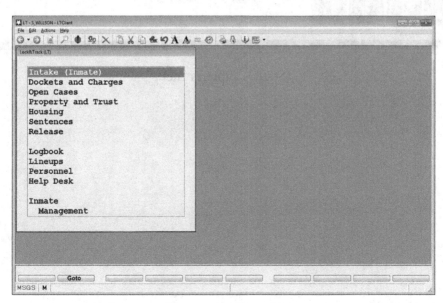

(Source: Locktrack)

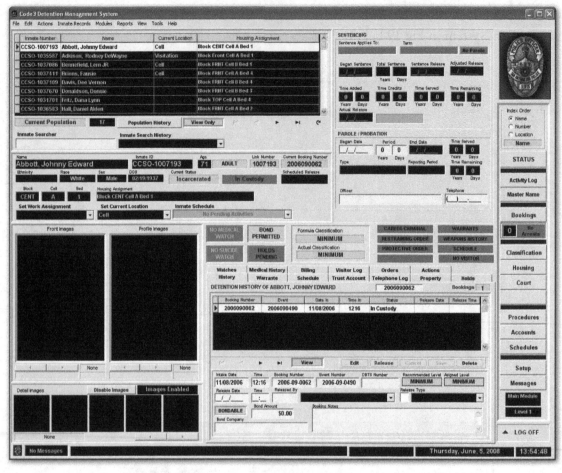

(Source: capterra Inc)

C. VIOLENT CRIMES

In fact violent crimes are murder, assault, rape, robbery, and burglary. It is paradoxical that in spite of its gruesome and uncanny nature, murder usually captivates man's attention more than all other crimes. Of course, this concern can be explained by the high value that all human societies attach to life. Similarly, this explains the conspicuous position of notoriety occupied by murder crimes in the hierarchy of violent crimes. In spite of its gruesome nature, perpetrators of the act seemingly do delight in the unsavory reputation earned in the commission of such acts. Such is the experience that serial killers and terrorists get when they commit series of murders or massive killings of innocent people respectively.

i. Degree of Prevalence

While there is a palpable reduction in the rate of domestic violent crimes in the United States nowadays as reflected by the statistics presented below, there is a serious rise in terrorism both at the domestic and international levels. Since the birth of Al-Qaeda followed by the bombing of the World Trade Center in New York on September 11, 2001, terrorism regained unprecedented strength worldwide. Such a revival is reinvigorated by the teaching of fundamentalist doctrines of Islam that incite jihadist militancy against US foreign policies. Their particular target and objective is to destroy Western education and civilization, *"Boko Haram"*. Their goal is to create Islamic states all over the world and convert everyone irrespective of race or origin to Islam through force of arms. In order to attain prominence and hopefully achieve their goals, their militants often resort to massive killing of innocent people. Christians are their special target, which they cynically label as infidels. Since 9/11, the US government more forcefully reorganized its forces and got prepared to combat this form of violent crime. A lot of resources ranging from finances, human, logistics, and legislation are being deployed to combat it. But how successful is this national effort in preventing this evil? Of course, a lot of success is being registered. A lot of homegrown terrorist plots have been uncovered and thwarted by the forces assigned with this duty. Speedy responses and interventions to the few successful acts followed by investigations and arrests have been registered.

However, far from being pessimistic, it is evident that neither heavy budgetary investment in the area of crime control and prevention by the government nor strong legislation can actually stop violent crimes or murder in particular. Determined criminals have always gotten their way though they always get caught and indicted for their offenses. An interesting paradox in the criminal justice system is the fashionable display of legal expertise in the courts by defendants of violent crimes and their defense attorney to edge their way out of the case and go free. They would tactfully invoke constitutional protections and other legal protective provisions of the law to strike down the murder charges of which they are genuinely guilty, thereby making a mockery of the case.

The example of Gregory *Wayne* (defendant) in *Commonwealth of Virginia v. Gregory Wayne* [18] is a case in point. After pleading guilty to the murder of Lambrecht, Gregory still tactfully hoped to go free by employing all legal expertise in his defense. He and his defense counsel resorted to the very constitution and the law that he had violated for protection. He invokes those areas like the Miranda rights that are intended to protect the innocent suspect against self-incrimination as well as the right to speedy trial, a constitutional protection intended to ensure a fair trial. This situation pushes one to question whether the law, in an effort to protect the innocent, has not actually granted the real offender the very tools to shelter himself against the application of justice.

ii. Violent Crimes Trends

In general, violent crime rate in the United States, especially homicide, has persistently indicated a downward trend in the last two decades (1990-2010) as shown in the two graphs below extracted from the Bureau of Justice Statistics (BJS) and Arizonawatch.com respectively. By 1973 violent crimes totaled about 3.6 million. Within an interval of ten years in 1982 it rose slightly above 4 million. It experienced a drop in 1986 and started rising again to an apex in 1994. From then it has maintained a steady drop right up to 2010 (fig. 21). Unfortunately, no reasons have been advanced for the direct cause of this drop.

---

[18]   *Commonwealth of Virginia v. Gregory* is a 1998 criminal case held in the Circuit Court of Virginia in Chesterfield County in which a certain Gregory Wayne was charged with capital murder, robbery, and two counts of use of a firearm in the commission of a felony. In the remaining trial he was charged for burglary, grand larceny, and vandalism. See a review of this case further down in this book.

Fig. 20 NATIONAL TRENDS IN VIOLENT CRIMES FROM 1973-2008

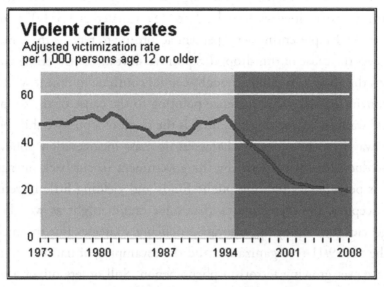

(Source: Bureau of Justice Statistics-BJS)

NB Statistics used in designing this chart took account of the victims of the 9/11 terrorist bombing of the World Trade Center in New York.

Fig. 21 NATIONAL TRENDS IN VIOLENT CRIMES 1984-2010

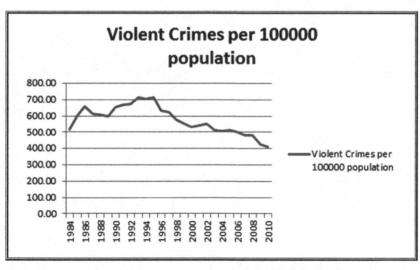

(Source: Arizonawatch.com)

Contrariwise within the same period, national prison population (see fig. 22 below) continued to witness a steady increase up to 2009 when it started to drop. Remarkably State and Federal Corrections facilities witnessed a decrease estimated at 1,571,013 convicts in 2012 from 1,598,783 in 2011 representing a 1.7 percent according to reports from Bureau of Justice Statistics. Whatever the cause of this drop, this positive shift in the US crime rate constitutes a source of relief to the American public though sceptics continue to take it with a pinch of salt as there is no convincing statistical evidence pointing to the cause of the drop. While many Americans would want to believe that this drop is the result of a positive shift by the Criminal Justice System away from its previous characteristic mass incarceration policy, others think that it might be due to fiscal concerns by the government to cut back on national budget, in an area that is perpetually draining public funds and yielding little in return. Whatever the opinion of sceptics, the fact remains that some credit might as well be given to law enforcement agencies for employing innovative policing strategies (for instance Community Policing) and the post 9/11 re-organization and the revamping of national security strategies in response to the ever growing terrorism phenomenon. Still others might also want to give credits to the governments of conservative states like California, Arkansas and Texas that started to realize as Professor Joan Petersilia[19] puts it "gotten the message that locking up a lot of people doesn't necessarily bring public safety."

---

[19]   New York Times: US Prison Populations decline, Reflecting New Approach to Crime; Erica Goode, July 2013

Fig 22: STATE AND FEDERAL PRISONS POPULATION STATISTICS, 1925-2012

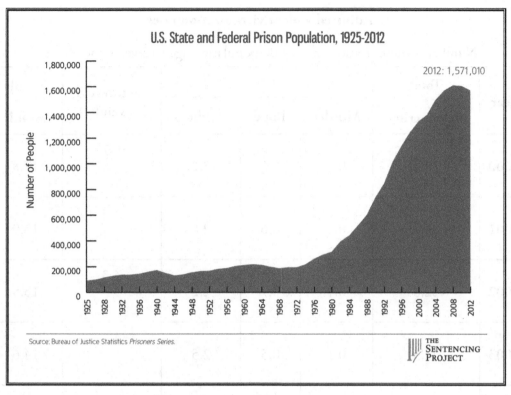

Source: Bureau of Justice Statistics.

The following figures obtained from the FBI's *Uniform Crime Report* validate the steady decline in the rate of violent crimes indicated in the charts above from the Bureau of Justice Statistics and the Arizonawatch. Homicide data were calculated from the FBI's *Uniform Crime Reports*. Homicide rates for 2004 are estimated based on 2004 preliminary annual release data.

Table 3 ADJUSTED VIOLENT VICTIMIZATION RATES

Adjusted violent victimization rates					
Number of victimizations per 1,000 population aged 12 years and above.					
Year	Total violent crime	Murder	Rape	Robbery	Aggravated assault	Simple assault
2000	27.4	0.1	0.6	3.2	5.7	17.8
2001	24.7	0.1	0.6	2.8	5.3	15.9
2002	22.8	0.1	0.7	2.2	4.3	15.5
2003	22.3	0.1	0.5	2.5	4.6	14.6
2004	21.1	0.1	0.4	2.1	4.3	14.2

Source: FBI's Uniform Crime Reports

This drop might be attributed to the increase in funding of the criminal justice agencies notably the Police, Corrections, and the Judiciary that occurred between 1982 and 2006 as indicated in fig. 23 below.

Fig: 23 US—CRIMINAL JUSTICE COST TIMELINE

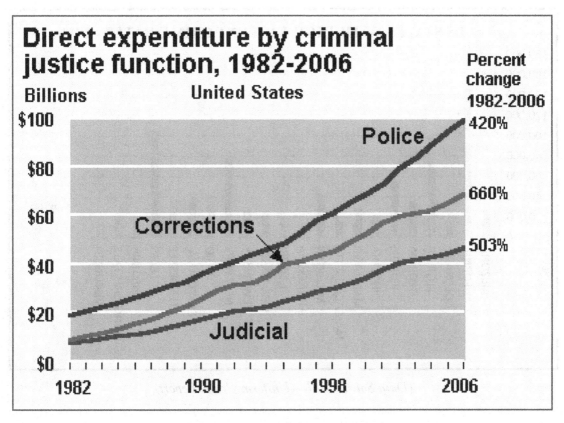

(Source: Bureau of Justice Statistics)

With budgetary increases in the Criminal Justice agencies indicated in fig 23 above, we might infer that a resultant increase in the recruitment, training, staffing and deployment of police officers as well as personnel in the related criminal justice agencies coupled with innovative planning and crime control strategies actually contributed to produce a deterrent effect on crimes, thereby producing a corollary drop in prison population mentioned above. However in spite of this drop, the US still ranks first in the world with the highest crime rate and highest prison population. Up to 2011 violent crime statistics still remain very high in some US states as indicated in the bar chart here below. Four states, namely California, Texas, Florida, and New York, still rank highest on the chart for violent crimes. It's worth noting that only states with crime rates above five thousand are represented on this chart.

Fig. 24 VIOLENT CRIME STATISTICS BY STATES, 2011

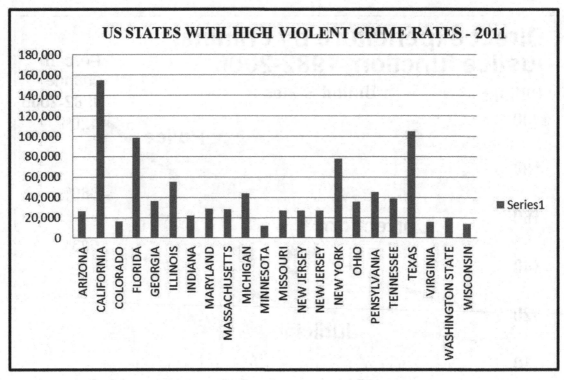

(Data Source: FBI—Uniform Crime Report)

iii. National Youth Violence

Youth violence refers to violence perpetuated by persons of both sexes between the ages of ten to twenty-four years. The national violent-crime arrest rate among youths in the United States was 519.6 males and 118.5 females per 100,000 populations in 2009 (fig. 25 below). Specifically, males between the ages of fifteen to nineteen registered a very high rate of 730.3 per 100,000 populations. Meanwhile, females of the same age range registered a lower rate of 151.0 per 100,000 populations.

Fig. 25 NATIONAL STATISTICS OF YOUTH VIOLENT OFFENSES

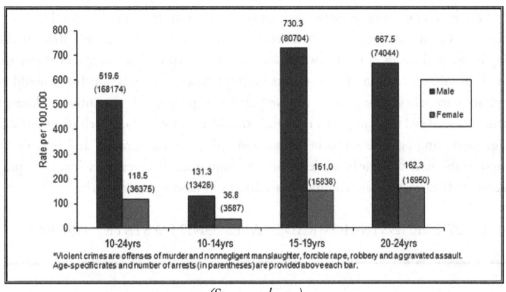

(Source: cdc.gov)

Fig. 26 NATIONAL STATISTICS OF YOUTHS WITH NONFATAL ASSAULT-RELATED INJURIES

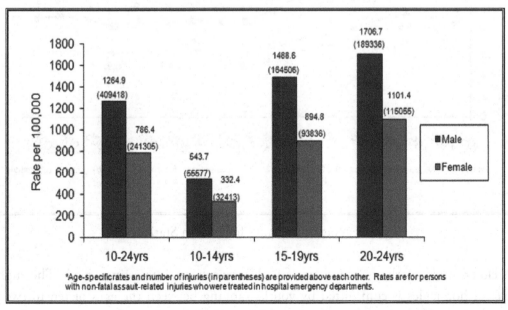

(Source: cdc.gov)

Youth violence creates a very serious emotional, social, and economic strain on families and the nation as a whole. It is unfortunate that homicide in particular remains the leading cause of death among young persons aged ten to nineteen in the United States. Figures from the National Center for Health statistics reveal that 650,723 young people (fig. 26 above) ranging between the ages of ten to twenty-four years were treated in emergency departments for non-fatal injuries resulting from assaults in 2009. These statistics hopefully should serve as inspiration to policy makers to formulate policies or prevention programs to address this unfortunate social evil that continues to engulf American communities. Such programs should envisage promoting positive social behaviors and strengthening families and making them more responsible over the youths while creating communities that eschew violence and prevent easy access to firearms that are commonly acquired and used by these youths.

Fig: 27 TRENDS IN HOMICIDE RATES, UNITED STATES, 1991-2007

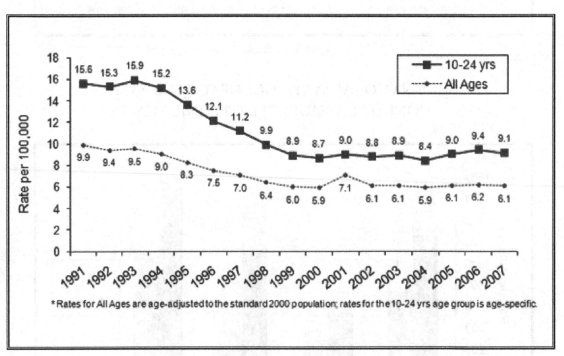

(Source: National Center for Health Statistics)

A closer study of the above chart (fig. 27) reveals an interesting trend. The highest number of homicides is committed by youths ranging between the ages of ten to twenty-four years with the highest peak between 1993 and 1994. What factors account for this trend and specifically this period in time? Anyone familiar with the American socio-political environment would surely admit that there is a very high prevalence of drug sale and consumption, easy access to weapons, and violent gang activities among youths in the streets and in schools including colleges. The Second Amendment of the US Constitution—I quote, **"A well-regulated Militia being necessary to the security of a free State, the right of the people to keep and bear Arms shall not be infringed"**—expressly provides the citizens the right and freedom to bear arms. This provision accounts for the proliferation of firearms and the ensuing violence. Gang associations and activities that most often create conflicts are boosted by easy access to weapons and drug consumption and sale. All these factors predispose youths to violence that often leads to homicide. The clue as to why the rate of homicide committed by youths of ages ten to twenty-four was particularly higher between 1993 and1994 is not visible. The analysis of the above chart also reveals another trend. Youths of ages ten to twenty-four years consistently committed a higher number of homicides than persons of all other ages within the same period, 1991-2007. A very positive trend, however, is also revealed. The homicide rates for both age groups consistently experienced a downward trend from 1995 to 2007. It fell from 15.9 to 9.1 for ten to twenty-four years and from 9.9 to 6.1 for all other ages between 1993 and 2007. This is a very encouraging indicator. What accounted for this fall should be the concern of politicians and policy makers if they hope to maintain this downward trend and keep the youths and society in general safety.

Though it is difficult to state with certainty what directly contributed to this fortunate drop in the isolated violent crime rate, we may rightly point to those factors that in normal circumstances would influence crime control and prevention in general. I am referring here to national crime control efforts in policy formulation, effective implementation of these policies by the different agencies concerned (FBI, CIA, DEA, ATF, as well as the local law enforcement agencies), the criminal justice system, and the allocation of the necessary resources by the US Congress. All these factors in spite of their shortcomings surely contributed to lower isolated violent crime rate in one way or the other during this period in time. Can this joint effort be sustained in order to keep the American society safe? Yes, if the will to do so is there and all efforts are made to sustain it. Unfortunately, when we think that one form of crime is subsiding here, another form shoots up. A case in point is terrorism that continues to prove the insolvable nature of the crime phenomenon.

Terrorism, a more serious form of violent crime that aims at inflicting massive casualties, revealed a renewed momentum in the United States since April 19, 1995, with the bombing of the Oklahoma Federal Building[20] followed by the September 9, 2001, bombing of the World Trade Center[21] in New York. It has since then persistently gained notoriety. Although the main perpetrators of this form of crime are mostly foreign enemies of America and their activities mostly planned and carried out against American interest abroad, it is actually mind-boggling to note that some Americans are also involved in it with the homeland being their most favored target.

Although everyone potentially is a victim of crime, some minority groups in society are more often susceptible to some categories of crimes than others. Women, for instance, are by their sex more susceptible to violent crimes of rape that most often end with the murder of the unfortunate victim. This type of violent crime, like the rest of crimes in general, has within the last decade fortunately experienced a steady decline as indicated in the following statistics obtained from the Bureau of Justice Statistics.

Fig: 28 US RAPE RATES BETWEEN 1973-2003

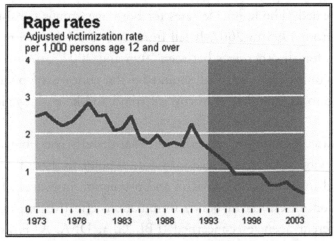

(Source: National Center for Health Statistics)

---

[20] The Oklahoma Federal Building bomb attack that took place on the nineteenth of April 1995 was a domestic terrorist act planned and executed by a certain Timothy McVeigh. This attack killed 680, including children under six years of age. It also injured 680 people and damaged 320 buildings and eighty-six cars within the vicinity.

[21] The World Trade Center terrorist attack of September 9, 2001, is often referred to as 9/11. It was a well-coordinated terrorist attack planned and executed by an Islamic jihadist group known as Al-Qaeda with Osama Bin Laden as leader. The terrorists used four hijacked airplanes to attack and destroy the twin buildings that made up the World Trade Center in New York and the Pentagon. It killed more than three thousand people, including passengers and crews of these planes. Bin Laden was, after more than ten years of this attack, found and killed by US Navy Seals in his hideout in Pakistan in May 2011.

iv. Prevention Programs

Like everywhere else, violence constitutes a serious public health problem in the United States. It affects people in all stages of life, from infants to the elderly. According to statistics obtained from the Center for Disease Control (CDC), in 2009 about 16,800 people were victims of homicide, and nearly 37,000 took their own lives. The number of violent deaths tells only part of the story. Many more survive violence and are left with permanent physical and emotional scars. Violence also erodes communities by reducing work productivity, decreasing property values, and disrupting social services. The Center for Disease Control through federal government funding is doing a lot to fight against not only diseases that cause deaths but also all sorts of violence including violent crimes. This center funds programs and initiatives that aim at preventing or reducing violence in the society. The following are some of the areas and programs being funded and sponsored by the CDC.

- Public Health Leadership Initiative (PHL)
- Domestic Violence Prevention Enhancement and Leadership Through Alliances (DELTA)
- Academic Centers for Excellence (ACE)
- National Violent Death Reporting System (NVDRS)
- Rape Prevention and Education (RPE)
- Striving To Reduce Youth Violence Everywhere (STRYVE)
- Violence Education Tools Online (Veto Violence)

As earlier stated, we cannot postulate with certainty the exact cause of this fortunate decline in violent crime rate. Without limiting our scope uniquely to the effort employed by the different agencies charged with criminal justice and crime control and prevention, we may also consider other contributing factors like alternative crime prevention methodologies or approaches and public policies. For instance, better training of law enforcement officials, preemptive policing, problem solving, and community policing. These new policing orientations and missions different from the traditional method of law enforcement and maintenance of order embraced in the early nineties obviously have contributed in the past decade to yield the above mentioned fruits. The contention whether capital punishment does produce any deterrent effect in potential homicide offenders remains potently controversial. Failing to have any palpable evidence to confidently confirm this assertion, Attorney General

Janet Reno[22] had this to say, **"I have inquired for most of my adult life about studies that might show that the death penalty is a deterrent, and I have not seen any research that would substantiate that point."** Meanwhile, Senator Orrin Hatch relying on scientific evidence as proof of the deterrent effect of capital punishment, honestly states thus, "All of the scientifically valid statistical studies—those that examine a period of years, and control for national trends—consistently show that capital punishment is a substantial deterrent." Such antithetical stances only help to heighten the controversy over death penalty as possible deterrent to criminality.

After carrying out an empirical study of US time-series data on the deterrent effect of capital punishment, Isaac Ehrlich[23] concludes that indeed capital punishment produces a deterrent effect on potential murders. Of course the result of his analysis was widely accepted in the United States even though it still remains controversial to many.

22 Skeptical Enquirer Magazine, July 2004, Capital Punishment and Homicide Sociological Realities and Econometric Illusions—Attorney General Janet Reno, January 20, 2000
23 The Journal of Criminal Law and Criminology, Capital Punishment and Deterrence: Conflicting Evidence, 1983 Northwestern University School of Law. Vol. 74, No. 3

PART V

CRIME CONTROL/ PREVENTION THEORIES

I. Utilitarian

The utilitarian theory contends that crime control can be achieved from three viewpoints:

- **Deterrence**
- **Rehabilitation**
- **Incapacitation**

With regards to deterrence, they contend that if criminal justice professionals (jurists and courts) could impose the right penalties on the right offenders for the right crime, this would deter criminals and consequently lead to crime reduction. As for rehabilitation, utilitarians believe that if therapeutic professionals (e.g., corrections) could apply appropriate techniques, this would lead to reduction in crimes. Meanwhile advocates of incapacitation believe that if criminal justice professionals could select the right people to be incapacitated, crimes would be reduced. In summary, utilitarians believe that the whole problem of crime control rests in the hands of criminal justice professionals. Criminal justice professionals are the only ones to take over the responsibility of crime control utilizing informed scientific input to prevent crimes in the society.

II. Neoclassicists

The neoclassicist contention is that criminology as a science cannot provide the required professional know-how that would lead to effective crime reduction. Crime reduction they believe falls within the realms of jurisprudence. Jurist professionals should develop a system of punishment that would help in crime reduction. Only a system of punishment developed by professional jurists and commensurate with the offenses can help in crime reduction. Neoclassicists very strongly disagree with the contention that communities should take informal initiatives in crime resolutions independent of the criminal justice system. For instance, serious offenses committed by young offenders or among school pupils or students should not be handled and resolved by school or college authorities in association with parents of the offenders or victims of the offense. Any serious crime committed whether within or outside of school premises by pupils or students should be referred to the courts where the deserved trial and punishment would be administered by the appropriate criminal justice professional or authority. Neoclassicists believe that community crime control produces two important risks: too much *leniency* or too much *oppression*. If the offender is treated with too much leniency, the purpose of punishment and deterrence would be defeated. Similarly, if on the other hand, the offender is treated too severely, the punishment would become oppressive and would produce a counter effect on deterrence and crime control. They believe that if left with community, justice would become not only inconsistent and unjust but essentially unpredictable because of lack of expertise knowledge in its application. Justice administered by professional jurists is systematic and well measured—neither less nor too much. My personal comment here is that the neoclassical perception of the criminal justice system is a purist one that is hardly practiced in real-life situations. This is so because in real practice there are circumstances where errors committed by some criminal justice professionals lead to the punishment of innocent people, while in other situations, real offenders walk away scot-free. Many reasons can be advanced to justify some of these errors. Just to name a few—the collection of evidence and preservation may be flawed resulting in the conviction of an innocent person or in the discharge of a real offender.

III. Liberal-Permissive

- ## Becker (1963)

Liberal-permissive theorists like Becker focused on the concept of labeling (i.e., name giving). They believe that crime is not so much the nature of the act than the label (name) assigned to it by society based on a system of rules and sanctions conceived by society and attributed to it. In brief, a crime is simply what society, based on its system of rules and sanctions, has decided to call it. Becker puts it thus: **"Deviance is not a quality of the act a person commits but rather a consequence of the application by others of rules and sanctions to an offender. The deviant is one to whom that label has successfully been applied; deviant behavior is behavior that people so label it."** The liberal-permissive concept touches on morality. What and who determines the "wrongness and rightness of any act"? What is right in the eyes of A may be wrong in B's eyes.

- ## Kitsuse (1962)

"Forms of behavior per se do not differentiate deviants from nondeviants; it is the responses of the conventional and conforming members of society who identify and interpret behavior as deviant which sociologically transform persons into deviants." Kitsuse in the above passage is affirming that it is not behavior (whether criminal or noncriminal) that makes the difference in people. Rather what makes the difference is the name (label) that conformists to social rules or conventions have decided to give those that commit crimes. Indeed, a crime is only bad depending on the person who perceives it. This perspective of crime only recalls to us the controversial concept of good and evil or the concept of morality and immorality. What is evil and what is good? What is moral and what is immoral? Are all these not just labels conceived by society? Is something necessarily evil because another person feels so? Or is what I consider good necessarily good to another person? The labeling-theory perspective of crime control actually contributed to fostering more research into criminology. It helped criminologists to develop the idea of tolerance and understanding of criminals. The labeling theory makes an appeal to society to have a different perspective from the ordinary about the criminal. It views the criminal more as a victim than an offender. It appeals for sympathy for the criminal/delinquent. According to this theory, society has sinned against criminals. Consequently, it requests society to leave the criminal alone. Crime or delinquency is just part of life and should be tolerated as such. This is a message to criminal justice professionals. Stay off criminality because it is just another aspect of life. After examining these three theoretical perspectives, we see an interesting display of concepts. While the utilitarians and neoclassicists are against community involvement in crime control in preference of jurist professionals, the liberal-permissive traditions are informing jurist professionals and community to stay off criminality with their system of punishment (Schur 1973). One question comes to mind. When neoclassicists argue in favor of community neutrality in crime control, are they not in a way encouraging criminality since professionals cannot do it alone? When liberal-permissive traditions call for hands-off crime control by professionals, are they not encouraging crimes? Crime control cannot be an issue of a simple unit. It can only be achieved through concerted and active participation by several forces: jurist professionals with their system of shaming and punishment on the one hand and through participation by a community of law-abiding citizens on the other. Most low-crime societies are those in which communities actively participate with professionals to handle their crime problems rather than handing them entirely to professionals and staying hands-off while watching them do it alone.

IV. The Marxist Theory

The Marxist theory contends that capitalist economies create a lot of social ills. For instance, capitalists' insatiable search for profit leads to the introduction of new technologies (machines) to increase mass production and output in business. This process creates massive layoffs of the proletariat or working class that is already disadvantaged in the production process through low wages. The application of this system has practically replaced or reduced the number of employment opportunities for the medium and lower class workers. This phenomenon is very perceptible in supermarkets or big shops like Giant, Safeway, Home Depot, Walmart, and others around neighborhoods in America. Human cashiers have virtually been replaced with self-service cashier machines that prepare bills when buyers scan their merchandise, receive payment, and produce receipts of payment to buyers from these shops. This situation creates a lot of unemployment while profiting the shop owners. The sequel is the creation of a class of unemployed, poor, and disgruntled masses or what Karl Marx calls a reserve army of the unemployed[24] and social stratification, class inequalities,

---

[24] Karl Marx described the class of unemployed masses as an "army of the unemployed."

unfair distribution of economic resources, and lack of opportunities for self-development. These forces doubtlessly constitute the main causes of criminality. This assertion is evidenced by the high crime rates in capitalist economies (America, Singapore, and Israel) as opposed to socialist Europe. For solution to this problem, the Marxist theory calls for the overthrow of capitalism and changes to class income inequalities.

V. Re-integrative Shaming Theory

Re-integrative shaming is a crime control method offered by criminologist Durkheim (1961) as a better alternative to the criminal justice system epitomized by imprisonment and characterized by repression. Re-integrative shaming can be explained simply as a system in which society disapproves in a very formal or informal way criminal or deviant behaviors. This social-disapproval process is accompanied by moralizing appeals that bring the individual to realize that his choices violate social norms. An individual cannot claim to be morally upright when he places only his own interest first in the choices he makes in his social interaction with others in his community. Such moral appeals would awaken the individual's conscience to realize the shame embodied in exercising his autonomy in such a way that tramples on the rights of others in the society. Further, this moral-education process offers the individual the chance to prove his innocence or admit his guilt, express his remorse, and seek pardon for his offenses. If not satisfied, he is given the chance to challenge the legitimacy of the social norm that he is accused of violating. In conclusion, re-integrative shaming offers the individual the opportunity for social re-integration. Durkheim views the traditional crime control system typified by criminal law as repressive, brutal, and in violation of human dignity. He feels that this system does not work and needs to be discarded in preference to a social control system in the form of moralization. Durkheim contends that the claim of violation of social norm by criminal behavior does not justify the continuous application of the repressive and inhuman and immoral social control system (criminal law). In short, criminal law or the criminal justice system, according to Durkheim, is repressive and should be discarded as crime control policy option. **"Ideas and feelings need not be expressed through untoward manifestation of force, in order to be communicated. As a matter of fact such punishments constitute today quite a serious moral handicap. They affront a feeling that is at the bottom of all our morality, the religious respect in which the human person is held. By virtue of this respect, all violence exercised on a person seems to us, in principle, like sacrilege. In beating, in brutality of all kinds, there is something we find repugnant, something that** revolts our conscience—in a word, something immoral. Now, defending morality by all means repudiated by it, is a remarkable way of protecting morality. It weakens on the one hand the sentiments that one wishes to strengthen on the other." Durkheim believes that re-integrative shaming does not only make individuals responsible but also awakens their consciences to the negative effects of their criminal behavior to society and how much other citizens resent this behavior. This method, he believes, can produce the same crime control results without necessarily employing brutal means. Re-integrative shaming theory considers shaming a better social control policy against deviant behaviors. John Braithwaite puts it thus: **"In other words, shaming is a route to freely chosen compliance, while repressive social control is a route to coerced compliance."** He goes further to explain the difference between repressive social control (criminal law) and moralizing social control (re-integrative shaming) in the following words: "Repressive moral control, as by imprisonment, restrict our autonomy by forced limitation of our choices; moralizing social control restricts our autonomy by inviting us to see that we cannot be whole moral persons through considering only our own interests in the choices we make. We are shamed if we exercise our own autonomy in a way that tramples on the autonomy of others." But just how far shaming should go is the question. Shaming as recommended by Daniel Glaser should be re-integrative rather than constitute a stigma. Deviant behavior that is not criminal should neither be punished nor shamed publicly. When shaming is done in such a way as to avoid being a stigma and also when it respects human dignity, it promotes non-harmful behavior. John Braithwaite recommends that non-harmful deviance policy should be an acceptable norm in liberal societies. He also recommends informal social control (i.e., shaming) as a better means of controlling a harmful deviant person within local communities, schools, and families on social groupings instead of resorting to the repressive social control system applied by states. Community settings favor informal social control policies, which are less repressive than the criminal justice system.

PART VI

CRIME CONTROL POLICIES AND SOLUTIONS

PREVENTIVE POLICIES

After examining the causes or origins of crimes, the obvious question that comes to mind is, "How do we prevent crimes from happening?" In other words, is crime prevention a reality? Can crimes be totally prevented? The answer is certainly no! Total crime prevention is an idealistic concept. It might sound better to talk of crime control rather than total crime prevention. What crime control policies are available then for society? Let us examine the following:

a. Non-Law Enforcement Control Measures

For any crime control policy to be meaningful and effective, policy makers as a matter of necessity must take into consideration the political, economic, biological, and social equations of their society when formulating crime control policies. We saw earlier in this book how the political and socioeconomic systems strongly correlate with criminality. In short, how a nation is organized politically (i.e. territorial arrangement and administration taking into account variables like race, culture, language, religion), employment, how national wealth or resources are distributed, and how social services are distributed and provided practically affect the crime rate of every nation.

When narrow-minded politicians pigheadedly hang on alien concepts borrowed from colonialism like nationalism, territorial integrity, unity, loyalty, republicanism, and so forth to forcibly band together people who are naturally heterogeneous in race, culture, language, and religion without proper consultation, misunderstanding, enmity, hatred, and evil are bound to breed in the minds of the citizens. This may find vent in the form of crimes and other antisocial manifestations. It is no exaggeration that social democracies, like those operating in Europe, experience lower crime rates than capitalist democracies like America or like the autocratic regimes in most of Africa. Political systems that suppress basic human rights, freedom, and civil liberties of its citizens and overtax them only breed the germ of social deviance and criminality. Any political system that fails to properly organize and administer its national territory such that its citizens feel at home, freely associate, and interact socially without a lot of restraints and social hurdles placed on them only breeds the germ of criminality and disorder. Political systems that are operated on the basis of tribalism, favoritism, and mediocrity rather than on merit and equitable jobs and national wealth distribution only prepare fertile grounds for all forms of social deviance and criminality. Criminality and antisocial manifestations can be controlled through political systems that make its citizens feel at home by the following options:

- Proper political consultation with the citizens followed by territorial organization and administration acceptable to the citizens.
- Operating an equitable and fair distribution of its natural resources and wealth.
- Providing social services to its people impartially without attaching strings of political allegiance.
- Applying a merit based nondiscriminatory employment system and equitable wage system.
- Avoiding tribal or group patrimony systems in the allocation of jobs, social services (such as hospitals and schools), and other developmental projects (electrification, good roads, markets).

When national wealth is distributed in a manner that favors some particular groups or tribes more than others, this breeds the germ of evil, hatred, crime, and disorder. A political system that promotes and encourages politics of exclusion, mediocrity, favoritism, corruption, and embezzlement of public funds with impunity only breeds deeply rooted anger, evil, and criminal intents in the hearts of those sections of its population that are marginalized and left out in the cold. Capitalist systems that operate high income inequality while eschewing all socially oriented programs breed evil and potential disorder. A system that encourages the concentration of wealth in the hands of a tiny upper class is potentially evil. It breeds deeply rooted anger in the hearts of its citizens, the germ of violence, and the desire to revenge.

The imprisonment statistics of a nation are often a direct reflection of its crimes' rates. To illustrate this point better, let us examine these two scatter plots below analyzing income inequality in highly industrialized capitalist countries.

Fig. 29 SCATTERPLOT OF COUNTRIES WITH INCOME INEQUALITY

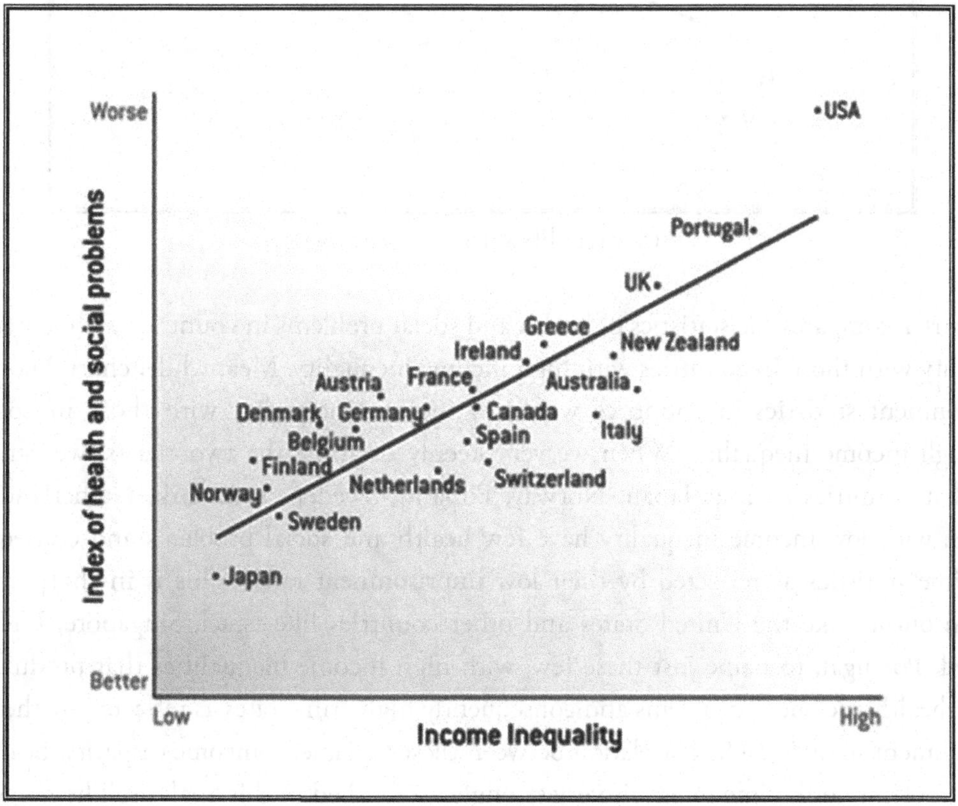

(Source: equalitytrust.org.uk)

Fig. 30 SCATTERPLOT INDICATING CORRELATION BETWEEN IMPRISONMENT RATES AND INCOME INEQUALITY

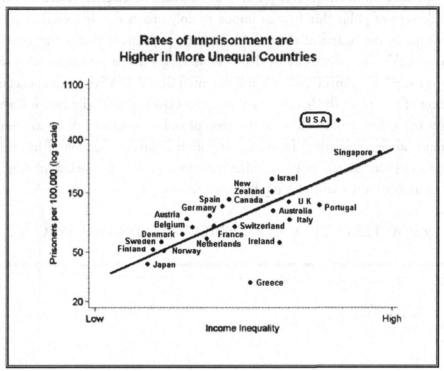

(Source: liberalslikechrist.org)

Chart 1 compares the statistics of health and social problems in countries with low income inequality with those in countries with high income inequality. Meanwhile, chart 2 compares imprisonment statistics in countries with low income inequality with those in countries with high income inequality. When we very keenly examine the two charts, we can safely infer that countries such as Japan, Norway, Finland, Sweden, Denmark, Netherlands, and so forth with low income inequality have few health and social problems and consequently low crime statistics as reflected by their low imprisonment rates. This is in sharp contrast with an outlier like the United States and other countries like Israel, Singapore, UK, New Zealand, Portugal, to name just these few, with high income inequalities that produce high rates of health and social problems and consequently high crime rates as reflected by their high imprisonment statistics. The correlation between these variables—income disparity, health and social problems, and crime rates—is very strongly established in this analysis. The remarkable position of the United States as a capitalist outlier in both analyses—income inequality and high imprisonment rates—seems to confirm Karl Marx's[25] consideration of capitalism as an economic system that breeds evil and crimes.

A system that fails to provide basic social services like good health, education, and opportunities for professionalization, good infrastructure (roads, markets, electricity, hospitals, water) to its people but rather taxes them out of every little business venture only predisposes its citizens to deviant activities and criminality. All these issues need to be well addressed if any nation hopes to have its national crime rate reduced. With regards to the biosocial equation, a nation needs to provide programs that keep the youths and teenagers occupied even after school. Statistics have proved that most unwanted pregnancies occur among teenagers and youths between the ages of fifteen to thirty years. Most criminal gangs are made up of youngsters between the ages of fifteen to thirty. And all these stem from frustration with the socioeconomic and political organization of the state.

b. Long-Term Crime Control Measures

Here below are some long-term crime control measures that policy makers may consider when formulating policies in this regard:

- Governments need to provide prenatal classes and health-care services to the communities to assist potential pregnant mothers.
- They need to train more nurses and organize prenatal monitoring services to would-be mothers. This will help to detect, control, and clear those developmental abnormalities associated with newborns.
- They need to provide pediatrician services to newborns and other children. These services and programs will help to clear or prevent some of the physical or cognitive abnormalities associated with poor parenting of children that at a later age predisposes them to antisocial behaviors and criminality.

---

[25] Karl Marx (1818-1883) was a German. His works inspired revolutionary communism that resulted in the foundation of many communist regimes in the twentieth century. One remarkable analysis of his economic theory is the consideration that capitalist profit is built on surplus value accumulated through exploitation of the proletariat.

- They need to institute skill classes right from high school to enable teenage children to acquire skills necessary in caring and bringing up healthy children.
- They need to provide community assistance to helpless teenage or adolescent mothers to prevent parental rejection of children.
- Educate mothers on the importance of prenatal diet to enable healthy growth of children.

c. Short-Term Crime Control Measures

The following short-term measures may also be helpful in crime control if instituted and followed up appropriately:

- Provide extracurricular activities or programs to occupy teenagers and youths.
- Prevent them from having access to street drugs.
- Control and prevent them from having easy access to lethal weapons (firearms).
- Reduce their access to violent movies, videos, and TV shows that glorify violence.
- Reduce their access to rap music that praises or incites to violence.
- Provide them opportunities for employment in cities, towns, and villages.
- Reduce chances of teenagers becoming single family parents.

d. Treatment Programs

While some social scientists like Wright and Decker[26] continue to grapple with the causes of crime, others attempt to reflect on treatment programs as alternative solutions to the crime issue. It is with this preoccupation in mind that Samenow[27], pushes further to applied theory by proposing concrete alternative programs to existing crime control and correctional

---

[26]   Wright and Decker; 1996, <u>Burglars on the Job</u>: street Life and residential Break-ins; UPNE, Boston
[27]   Samenow:1984. <u>Inside the Criminal Mind</u>, Crown Publishing Group.

methods. As if admitting total weakness in the development of preventive measures for criminality, he resorts to treatment as the sole remedy. Evidently the solution to criminality would be provided less by abstract or pure theorizing (Frank and Hagan 1986)[28] than by applied theory whose findings should foster crime control policies.

Samenow is less concerned with delving into the criminal's psyche to develop causes for his actions. Convinced that criminality is inherent in man's nature and operated on choice (free will), Samenow's concern is what to do with the criminal already in his state of criminality, hence, his devoted concern about offender treatment. He believes in the offender acknowledging his acts and submitting himself to treatment. In this wise, he develops and proposes a method of treatment of offenders. His proposal of an *open community correction system* solely for willing non-career criminals is quite an impressive treatment approach. He envisions this to be operated on the basis of a *probation system* granted by the courts. From his probation, the offender would attend on-campus *rehabilitation programs*. Successful graduates from the system would gain back full community life. Impressive as this proposal sounds, it however raises a number of questions. What would the system do with the career offenders that are beyond rehabilitation? Just keep them to continue eating on the system without any sort of economic return? Does he foresee the incapacitation or elimination system for them?

Samenow seemingly fails to make a pronouncement on this. What difference does it make with the present system of life sentence if career offenders are to be kept indefinitely locked up? Fostering the theory that criminality is inherent in man's nature without any in-depth exploration and support lacks strength of argument and tends to dismiss his theory. Whatever the case, his rather simplistic or outright rejection of other theories of criminality in favor of his alone sounds academically conservative. Every human behavior is influenced by associative motivating factors. As such, it appears not only unempirical but out-rightly wrong to pin an act to a single cause. Whatever his views on this, Samenow is not precise on how his system would affect criminality in general, let alone help prevent it. As for Wright and Decker, their research, excellent as it appears, remains pure theory, neither offering treatment nor postulating specific crime prevention policies.

---

[28] Frank and Hagan,1986. Introduction to Criminology: Theories, Methods and Criminal Behavior, Library of Congress Publication. Applied theories, as opposed to pure, make practical explanations that may guide existing policies in any research undertaking.

PART VII

CRIME DETERRENCE

I
n spite of abundant and modern technological resources available for use by law enforcement agencies, intelligence services, and all other forces concerned with criminal justice, deterring the professional and sworn criminal or terrorist remains an insurmountable feat. When one plot is uncovered today in one region, another is either being hatched or ready to be carried out the next day in another area. Scarcely does our applause for a successful uncovering of one plot subside than another criminal act is hatched or carried out elsewhere. The massive production and uncontrollable interstate and international circulation and easy sale of arms, drugs smuggling and consumption, religious fanaticism, selfish motivated politics, and ideological conflicts, have all contributed immensely in one way or the other to render the entire world extremely dangerous and unsafe. No one nation or region of the world seems to be spared by this monster of crime.

All forces concerned with criminal justice administration seem overwhelmed and helpless by multiform criminality and terrorism. The criminals and terrorists virtually have become the masters and are dead determined to take over control of society. The bombing of the World Trade Center on 9/11 in America speaks clearly for itself. Criminality and terrorism in particular actually beg for a serious reflection on the effectiveness of deterrence and methods of prevention. An ounce of prevention, as commonly said, is worth more than a pound of cure. This is the spur for all reflection on crime deterrence.

In an attempt to examine the different concepts of deterrence, we will see how the public perceives and feels about crime deterrence. We will also examine whether the effectiveness of crime deterrence can be measured, police methods of crime deterrence and how effective they are, why the criminal justice agencies should not bear the blame for killing crime deterrence, governments' efforts in crime deterrence, and public expectations of the criminal justice system.

a. What Is Crime Deterrence

To deter[29] means "to discourage or restrain from acting or proceeding through fear or doubt." Other synonyms are to: to prevent, to stop, to hinder, to dissuade, to check. Crime deterrence thus is the dissuasive or restraining effect produced in a potential offender by some external threat or potential threat of punitive action taken against him or some force exerted on him. In fact, it is a psychological process that takes place within an individual (potential criminal) producing a visible outcome to the observer. For instance, police presence and the threat of arrest normally produce a deterrent effect in criminals. The threat of court sentence of imprisonment produces a deterrent effect in some criminals. The severity of prison sentences, for example, twenty years, may produce a greater deterrent effect in some potential criminals than a simple two-year sentence. Besides being a psychological process, crime deterrence could also by extension, be considered as the collective measures or policies intended to produce restraining effects in potential criminals.

b. Conceptual Considerations

Law-abiding behavior is produced and sustained by the formal threat of legal sanction. This is what the fundamental concept of deterrence holds. The institution of social constructs like criminal law is a collective convention aimed at deterring crimes. Deterrent measures can be achieved in a short or long term depending on which crime preventive policy is implemented. Whether short—or long-term, deterrent effects are expected to impact on the subject and prevent him/her from committing a crime. Our concern here is less with the type of deterrence than with its effectiveness as a crime prevention policy.

---

[29] Webster's encyclopedic unabridged dictionary of the English Language, New Revised Edition, Gramercy Books. New York.

Criminal law is essentially deterrent in nature and intent because it sets social rules of conduct and sanctions that go with their violation. Criminal justice, on the other hand, is punitive. It enforces the respect of the rules set by criminal law and applies corresponding sanctions to defaulters. It is, however, assumed in their application that sanctions would produce a carryover effect of deterrence on the defaulters. This is where the conservative idea of severity of sanction as guarantee of deterrence intervenes. But does the certainty or severity of punishment actually produce a deterrent effect? Is crime deterrence achievable?

James Q. Wilson and Richard Herrnstein[30] in their rational choice theory consider crime deterrence as a psychological process that involves weighing the costs and benefits of the act before commission. **"At a given moment a person can choose between committing a crime and not committing it."** This theory holds that when there is a high risk of arrest and punishment, the offender refrains from the act. In this case the potential offender has been deterred by the feasible threat of punishment. But when the risk is low, the offender commits the act. Implicitly this low level of risk produces no deterrent effect in the subject. Unfortunately, not every criminal rationalizes on his/her act before commission. This theory cannot be considered exclusive in that an insane criminal for instance, never rationalizes on his/her actions. An insane criminal acts more on instincts/impulse than on reason due to his/her state of health. This assertion is strengthened by the inclusion of the insanity defense provision in the criminal justice system. Thus, the risk or severity of sanction cannot produce any deterrent effect in an insane criminal.

c. Public Perception of Deterrence

General public opinion perceives crime deterrence as not yielding the required results. Before and particularly after the unfortunate bombing of the World Trade Center on September 11, 2001, the entire American public appeared rather overcome by the magnitude of a seemingly ever-growing crime rate. Seeing its hopes for a safe society dashed to the bare floor by daily horrendous acts of homicide or incidents of kidnap followed by cold-blooded killings, people became imprisoned in abject fear of victimization. For instance, the Beltway sniper attacks of October 2002 widely spread fear of victimization among Americans. Amplified by the media, public opinion was rife with anger, accusations, and blame of policy

---

[30] Samuel Walker. <u>Sense and Non-sense about Crime and Drug</u>, 2001 Wadsworth, "Putting Severity of Punishment back in the deterrence package"

makers and particularly those agencies charged with crime control and prevention as the death toll continued to rise while the culprits were still at large.

A closer study of the US crime index per 100,000 inhabitants in the chart below reveals in average a steady increase that ranges from approximately 1,888 crimes in 1960 to 5,250 in 1996, with highest peaks of approximately 6,000 recorded in 1981 and 1992. The crime rate in 1960 had by 1996 grown to 317 percent. The index of crime statistics covers the period from 1960 to 2000. This statistics cover the following categories of crimes: aggravated assault, murder, rape, property crimes, robbery, burglary, larceny-theft, and vehicle theft. Remarkably, from 1993 it started experiencing a drop (fig. 30) that has continued till today.

Fig. 30 US CRIME INDEX STATE STATISTICS FROM 1960-2000

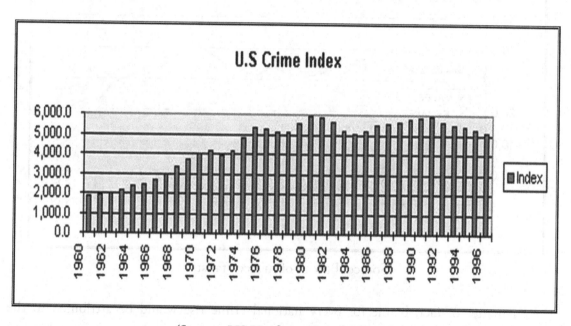

(Source: US Uniform Crime Report)

What explains this average steady rise in the US crime rate from 1960 to 1981 apex followed by a drop in 1985 and another steady rise to the 1992 apex? In fact, many factors may account either individually or collectively for these variations in the crime rate.

Fig. 31 VIOLENT CRIME RATES BY GENDER

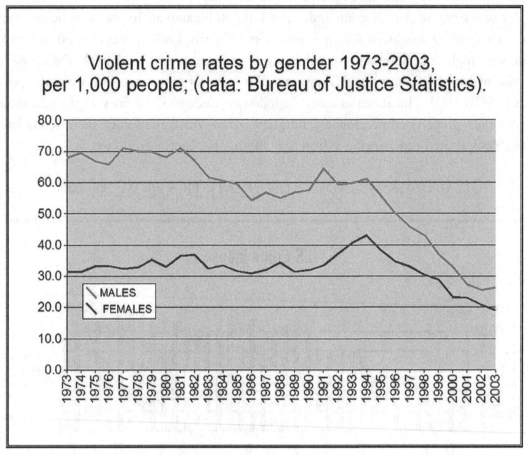

(Source: Bureau of Justice Statistics)

As a matter of fact, blame for every national crime rise would be attributed to the politicians. Firstly, politicians would bear the blame for failing to regulate gun ownership and use or failing to put the right criminal justice professionals in place to formulate good security policies that would deter crimes or terrorist acts. The US government's failure to regulate gun sale and purchase makes America occupy the highest position among countries with high gun ownership. The *Washington Post* small-arms survey statistics below show the position the United States occupies among these countries. (See figure 32 below.) There is no doubt that unregulated gun ownership would result in many guns in the hands of lawless people in the streets who would in turn use them in committing crimes.

Fig. 32 COUNTRIES WITH HIGHEST GUN OWNERSHIP

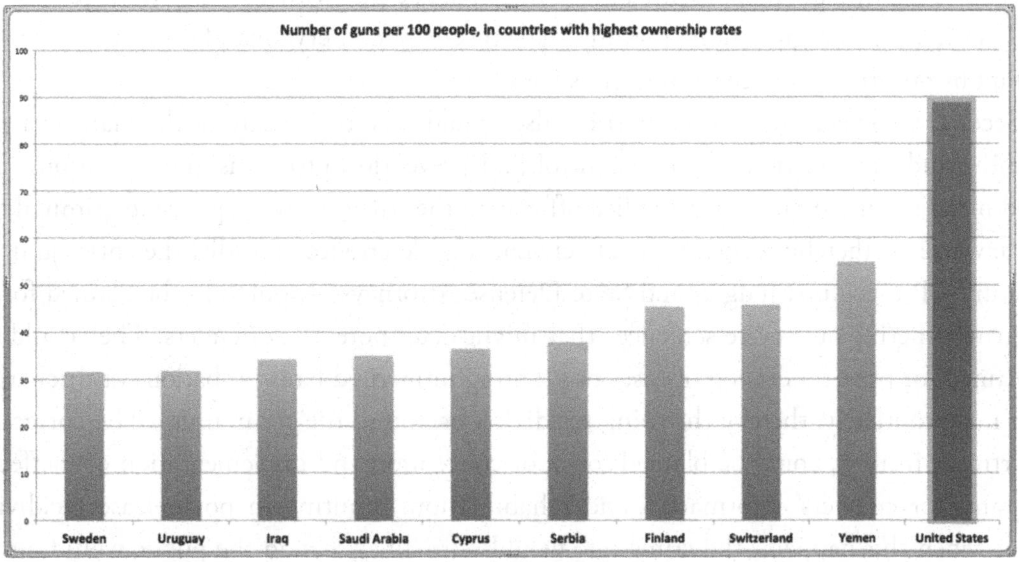

(Source: Small Arms Survey; Max Fisher / *Washington Post*)

In spite of the rise in the US domestic violent crimes[31] involving the use of firearms and the deaths of so many innocent people and schoolchildren, it has been difficult for government to enact regulations that could place restrictions on current easy sale of guns without serious security background checks of potential buyers. Most gun manufacturers and powerful lobbyists at the level of Congress have often stood in the way of any sort of legislation that would jeopardize their booming gun businesses. Remarkably, the National Rifle Association (NRA) has deployed all resources to impede all genuine efforts by good-intentioned liberal politicians to formulate restrictive policies or enact laws that would restrict the purchase of guns with high-capacity ammunition magazines. Americans' freedom to bear or own firearms is inherently historical and statutory. Born from the ashes of tyrannical Europe in the 1760, the citizens of the new nation (America) became so conscious of the price of their freedom that they would never let any historical repetition where a government would trample on the rights of its people. That is why conservative ideologists that stand strongly against these restrictive policies often quote the Second Amendment of the Constitution (the right for Americans to

---

[31] The Sandy Hook Elementary School shooting in Newtown, Connecticut, on December 14, 2012; the Sikh Temple shooting, Oak Creek, Wisconsin, on August 5, 2012; the Aurora Colombia movie theater shootings by James Holmes on July 20, 2012, and so forth.

bear arms against tyranny), in defense of their vested interest. It is not uncommon to hear slogans like "Only a good man with a gun can stop a bad guy with a gun," "More guns defend our liberties," "More guns fight tyranny", advanced by conservative ideologists against any attempt by government to enact anti-guns laws.

Secondly, law enforcement authorities also would take their share of the blame for poor planning and organization of crime control and prevention programs and operations. This could mean failure to put enough police officers in the streets, slow response to criminal acts, and few arrests, thereby reducing the effectiveness of deterrence. Thirdly, the entire judiciary structure—Prosecutors, Judges, and State Defense Attorneys—would also be blamed for not adequately meting out severe sentences that might deter potential offenders. They could also be blamed for poor processing of cases or granting unmerited bails/probations or discharging cases inappropriately, thereby throwing recidivists back into the community. The corrections department in turn, could be blamed for poor conception and implementation of ineffective programs for convicts' reformation and rehabilitation, resulting in post-release recidivism. In fact when this happens, the crime rate would normally rise, and the public would put the entire criminal justice system to question.

Some public opinions might argue rightly that delays in the administration of justice due to the inclusion of bottlenecks into the trial system namely; plea bargaining, appeal, bail, and habeas corpus, reduce the effect of deterrence. The public also believes that state-paid public defense attorneys and above all, inadequate punishment diminishes the certainty of punishment, hence reducing the effect of deterrence. Conservative[32] opinions have been very vocal against the lack of severity in punishing criminals by the criminal justice system. The institution of the famous "Three Strikes Laws and you're out[33]" laws enacted in 1992 by some states (California) and approved by the federal government, the Violent Crime Control and Law Enforcement Act (VCCLEA) that became Public Law no. 103-322 in September 1994, the USA PATRIOT[34] Act of October 2001, and many other conferences held to review

---

[32]   Samuel Walker. Sense and Non-sense about Crime and Drug, 2001 Wadsworth, pages 18-21

[33]   The "Three Strikes laws" were originated in 1990 by some US states (California) and later on approved by the federal government. These laws mandated stiff sentences for third-time offenders with the intention of getting career criminals off the streets. The application of these laws soon became unpopular because it created a serious backlash. States soon started experiencing high demands for big budgetary allocations to keep the convicts with long sentences in prisons.

[34]   The USA PATRIOT Act of October 2001 enacted by Congress and signed into law by President George Bush was intended to deter and prevent crimes and terrorism. The intention of this law is insinuated in its acronym: "Uniting and Strengthening America by Providing Appropriate Tools Required to Intercept and Obstruct Terrorism."

strategies aimed at crime control and terrorist prevention, are all brain children of these concerns about the rising crime rate. All these structures put together certainly explain the downward trend in the crime rate since 1994 as shown in figure 32 above. The administration of criminal justice in spite of the effort deployed by governments and its professionals to speed up the processes, will inherently remain slow for the following reasons.

The complex structure of the criminal justice system with numerous actors and components, functions and structured/formal methods or processes of application of the law, and logistics (including external factors like time and budgets), all affect its effective administration and any effort to speed up its processes. When we take all these factors into consideration, delays in the administration of criminal justice become an inevitable oddity that a community must accept and cope with. However, it would be incorrect to conclude on this premise and blame the ineffectiveness of crime deterrence on the weaknesses of the criminal justice system alone without considering the offender's shortcomings too. In fact the criminal justice system as a whole experiences more realities than what meets the eye. Let us briefly examine some of the causes of delays in the trial process for instance, that practically reduce the effect of deterrence. What accounts for these delays, and how justified is this practice if deliberate?

The criminal justice system functions as a chain starting with the police officers who effect the arrest, the prosecutors that prepare the case files and determine whether to indict the suspects or not, the defense counsel (state and private defense attorneys) that must intervene in the trial process to uphold the fairness of the system, the judge, and finally the correction department that receives the convicts, and implements and enforces court decisions. The judicial process is thus very lengthy and loaded with numerous processes, legal hurdles, and interventions, namely; constitutional concerns, investigative processes, human rights and freedom issues, religious considerations, budgetary concerns, moral and ethical constraints, local and professional cults, and sometimes politics that unnecessarily interfere and delay it.

All constitutions framed on the principles of democracy, are mandatorily bound to provide for the protection of the rights of its citizens against abuse by administrative or political powers. These provisions are intended to check biases and unnecessary abuse of power on others by the people in positions of authority. In the US Constitution, for instance, the Fifth Amendment is an example of such a provision, intended to guarantee free and fair judgment before the law for all its citizens. Since perfection remains an ideal, it is not unusual to have innocent people punished while real offenders go scot-free. This may happen not necessarily from the judge's conscious ill will, but because some errors might have filtered unknown to him into the process, starting possibly with the arrest. When this happens, an innocent person is arrested by the police and charged for an offense he never committed. The main intent of these processes that look like bottlenecks in the system are purposely aimed at protecting the innocent.

In order to avoid this and render just justice, it has often been the practice to carry out a thorough investigation. This process of course, requires time and logistics consequently inducing delays. In other instances, we have witnessed human rights organizations as well as some political institutions or even nations, intervene in judicial processes, rejecting out-rightly a capital sentence passed on a guilty murderer and requesting for clemency. Their reason for the most part is based on issues of morality. It is senseless they argue, to take away one life as punishment for another already lost. When a person is executed for committing murder, two lives are lost instead of one. This reaction and reasoning of course, affect and delay judicial processes.

It is rightly believed and often stated that "justice delayed is justice denied." This mind-set holds strongly in that the intensity of a criminal act and the emotions aroused diminish with the passage of time, and the effect of punishment is lessened when administered later than sooner. A freshly committed violent crime usually solicits violent outbursts of emotions and tensions from the public and the victim's family. The public is always anxious for a quick judgment and severe punishment of the murderer. Everyone favors a swift and severe sanction of the offender. Unfortunately, this is not always the case. There are prescribed judicial processes that must be followed. If punishment were to be so swiftly meted to the culprit, it may produce some deterrent effect. Unfortunately punishment cannot be summarily meted out else it undermines the very essence of justice. On the other hand, when the judgment process intervenes with unnecessarily lengthy investigations and postponements of trials, the magnitude of the crime and impact reduces. Punishment loses its intensity and effect. Deterrent effect is thus reduced or totally killed.

d. Measure of Crime Deterrence

Measurement of deterrence is more or less a Herculean task. This is a very controversial aspect of deterrence that has solicited countless hypotheses. Neither politicians nor legislators who formulate policies or make laws respectively, nor criminal justice experts and law enforcement professionals who apply and enforce the laws, can boast of conceiving any method of measurement of deterrence. Similarly, not even criminologists who gamble with statistics of crimes to formulate theories and hypotheses on causes and prevention of crimes, have been able to advance convincingly substantive modalities for the measurement of crime deterrence in any specific social context. Indeed, most considerations are based on mere theories, speculations, and assumptions. The punishment or sanctioning of criminals has always aimed at achieving four main objectives namely: *punitive goals, retribution, deterrence,* and *rehabilitation.* The Machiavellian split by conservative and liberal ideologies over the notion of punishment, constitutes a curious phenomenon.

While conservative opinions for instance, believe in and advocate for severe punishment of offenders by way of stiff prison sentences like the Californian "Three Strikes Law"[35] as a measure of deterring crimes, liberals on the other hand argue against this approach and propose a softer prevention policy. Conservative opinions assume that the severer the sanction, the more deterrent would be the effect. Liberals dispute that the severity of sanction does not guarantee deterrence. Posing in favor of milder sanctions and other alternative programs, liberals believe that this might produce more deterrent effects on potential criminals. They believe that severe sanctions only perpetuate the recycling of crime by hardening criminals.

In his article entitled "Back with a Vengeance," Michele Cotton[36] contends that deterrence is achieved through punishment, which is a tool for social control. He believes that the threat of punishment serves as a disincentive that dissuades potential criminals from committing offenses. He makes a distinction between general and specific deterrence. Unfortunately, sanctions irrespective of their intensity have not been a useful deterrence to crimes. However, programs for the treatment of offenders such as juvenile reformatory schools, drugs and alcohol treatment, mental health—all alternatives to imprisonment—have in spite of their high cost been known to produce a long-term deterrent effect. Some people may prefer to term it *incapacitation* and not *deterrence* since it keeps potential criminals for a long time away from the community. And they claim that this indeed does not constitute a measure of deterrence because once back in the community, some of these individuals do continue to commit crimes.

Peter K. Manning,[37] writing on "The Preventive Conceit," contends that deterrence as conceived by Jeremy Bentham, a social theorist, is intended simply to serve as a means of reducing the use of vengeance, and also to increase more humane forms of legal control. He further states in reference to Gibbs (1995) and Nagin (1978), that measurement and conception of deterrence continue to pose serious challenges. Elsewhere in "Preventive

---

[35] Peter J. Benekos and Alida Merlo, Three Strikes and you're Out! The political Sentencing Game.

[36] Michele Cotton, <u>American Criminal Law Review</u> Fall 2000 v37 i4 p1313. "Back with a vengeance"

[37] Peter K. Manning, <u>American Behavioral Scientist,</u>" May-June 1993 v36 n5 p (639) "The Preventive Conceit"

Conceit" he affirms that **"a belief in the deterrent effects of arrest is a *conceit* because it is mental activity organized by a misguiding metaphor that animates policy and research."**

This difficulty in determining the measure of deterrence, he explains further, is due to our inability to record and sanction all violators—indeed our inability to determine which acts are effectively deterred and which are not. The fact that arrest rates do not really reflect the totality of violations or criminal acts, since many crimes go unreported and hence unsanctioned is a case in point. Elsewhere he states that deterrence as a policy is not specific as to its aims. He doubts whether it should be aimed at dissuading individual criminals or at reducing crime rate.

Punishment may not necessarily deter crime commission. It may on the contrary, serve as a stimulus for further crimes in career criminals. He suggests that applying other measures, such as those that affect the environment, modify the law, and reduce opportunities that predispose to crimes, may produce better deterrent effects. He proposes, as alternative to punishment, community-based programs that may produce long-term deterrence in potential criminals.

Stephen W. Baron and Leslie W. Kennedy,[38] in a study of homeless male street youths in Canada, realized that male youths in general fear legal sanctions. But this category of homeless male street youths was particularly not affected by any formal threat of punishment. This study revealed that their poor conditions, coupled with constant use of drugs and their association with peers of similar lifestyle (withdrawn from conventional society), greatly emboldened them, thereby reducing in them the fear of sanction. These youths were already deeply immersed in a lifestyle characteristic of drug addicts. Other youths not part of this group the research revealed, were however, affected by the threat of punishment and refrained from crime commission.

e. Deterrence and Severity of Sanction (The Death Penalty)

The death penalty is the most severe punishment often meted out for murderers. It is still carried out in a good number of states in the United States and other countries, although it often solicits a lot of controversies and protests by human rights organizations and activists against its continuous application. Public opinion polls in the case of a freshly committed murder, have always favored its application as equitable punishment for the offender.

---

[38]   Stephen W. Baron and Leslie W. Kennedy_Canadian Journal of Criminology, Jan 1998 v40 n1 p27-60. Deterrence and homeless male street youths. (Canada)

Characteristically, it is rarely immediately applied. This is because the process for trial in a murder case is deliberately long and full of openings intended to ensure fair trial.

The innocent person needs to be protected against wrongful execution else the system would tend to defeat its very purpose of creation, which is "fairness." For instance, plea bargaining, appeal, clemency, and bail constitute justifiable legal hurdles that give the offender ample opportunity to save himself in the case where he is innocent of the offense for which he is charged. For this reason, the death penalty is scarcely applied or it takes a long process to decide on it. These delays obviously tend to produce what some experts call thermodynamic effects when finally applied. However, they are justified in a democratic system so long as they are not abused.

When a murderer for instance, is finally slated for execution after several years of deliberation on his case, people tend to feel and express strong sympathy for him. Some public opinions would even accuse the judicial or political authorities that finally affirmed the judgment of cruelty or coldheartedness. Time has already eroded the sympathy for the victim or victims of this reckless murderer. The case of Timothy McVeigh is a good example. When this fellow was scheduled for execution for his heartless bombing of the Oklahoma Federal Building in April 1995, that caused the death of hundreds of people, including innocent nursery schoolchildren, some people including human rights activists, took to the streets in protest against his execution.

These people's sympathy for those victims, especially the innocent children, had already eroded. Timothy McVeigh's single life suddenly became more important in their minds than the lives of those hundred innocent children that he had cold-bloodedly killed in a single bomb blast. What effect did these protests marches produce in the minds of other potential criminals? Certainly not sympathy for the victims or their families left behind to mourn them. Of course, it only made him a hero and emboldened other criminals in their plans and resolve. Certainly no deterrent effect was produced in them. The proof is that McVeigh did not manifest any sort of remorse or regret for his act. Instead he cynically referred to the loss of those innocent children as collateral damage and firmly implied that his act was not regrettable. Implicitly, the death sentence passed on him had no deterrent effect. If the judges had pardoned and left him alive, he surely would have plunged into similar or even more devastating acts of violence than the first one. If death penalties actually produced any significant deterrent effect, then there would have been a serious reduction in murder rates, especially in the state of Texas where this is highly carried out. While failing to produce any sort of deterrence in other criminals, the death penalty at least produces a feeling of vengeance or retributive justice in the minds of the victim's families.

In Texas as in many other states in the United States where death penalties are still applied, neither this practice nor the certainty or severity of punishment, nor delayed judicial processes seem to produce any effect of deterrence in the criminal subjects. The case of Timothy McVeigh clearly reveals an interesting phenomenon. The effectiveness of crime deterrence differs from criminal to criminal. Indeed it is determined by the individual criminal's conscience or state of mind and rarely by any external factor such as arrest, sanction, and quick or delayed judicial process. A hardened professional criminal would not be affected by any of these factors. All or some of the above factors may affect an opportunistic criminal who feels a touch of conscience and remorse for his act and not a professional or hardened criminal.

Silvia M. Mendes and Michael D. McDonald,[39] writing on "Social policy: Evaluation, Punishment in Crime Deterrence," contend in reference to eighteenth-century classical theories that deterrence owes its strength on the certainty and severity of punishment. This in turn depends on a high probability of arrest and conviction. These social scientists further hold that the nature of the sentence increases the certainty and severity of punishment, which raises the prospective cost of crime commission. When the cost of commission is high (*certainty of punishment*), this produces a deterrent effect in the potential offender. Arrest and conviction become vain threats when criminals go unpunished. Simply reflecting on the idea that he may be arrested and imprisoned for an offense no matter how severe the would-be sentence might be, is not enough to dissuade a potential criminal. If there is no certainty that he would be surely arrested and convicted if he commits the offense, then he will go ahead and commit the act. Referring to a series of empirical studies from 1970, Ann Witte (1983) concludes that higher probability of arrest, conviction, and imprisonment (*certainty of punishment*) produces a more deterrent effect in a potential criminal than the length of imprisonment (*severity of sentence*). Quoting Daniel Nagin and Greg Pogarsky in her report, Valerie Wright in November 2010[40] affirmed that "punishment certainty is far more consistently found to deter crime than punishment severity, and the extralegal consequences of crime seem at least as great a deterrent as the legal consequences."

In an experiment carried out by Cassia Spohn and David Holleran[41] on the deterrent effect of imprisonment, they found out using data collected on offenders convicted on felony charges

---

39 Silvia M. Mendes and Michael D. McDonald, Policy Studies Journal, Winter 2001 v29 i4 p588(23).

40 Valerie Wright; "Deterrence in Criminal Justice": Evaluating Certainty vs. Severity of Punishment; 2010 Washington DC

41 Cassia Spohn and David Holleran. Criminology, May 2002 v40 i2 p329 (29)." The effect of imprisonment on recidivism rates of felony"

in 1993 in Jackson County, Missouri, that imprisonment did not affect recidivism rate in any way. That is, imprisonment did not produce any deterrent effect in the convicted offender. Further findings revealed that offenders who were convicted to prison terms had a far higher rate of recidivism than those placed on probation. It was also noticed that imprisonment produced more criminal tendencies in subjects with drug offenses than in other offenders.

Basing our argument on the above line of thought, it is obvious that the answer to the question as to whether deterrence is achievable remains controversial. No clear-cut standard of measurement of the degree of crime deterrence has been established. Firstly, it makes sense that first-time offenders who are never rearrested for a second offense whatsoever, may have been deterred by the fear of their previous arrest and sanctions. This remains pure assumption because many things might have intervened to save them from re-arrest or detection after committing a second offense on release. For instance, it is possible that the victim of a second offense by the same person might have feared reprisal and did not report the act to the police, or the offender actually went undetected and hence was not arrested by the police.

If arrest were to be the measure of the effectiveness of deterrence, then how can we in this particular case evaluate it when actually a second offense was committed even though the offender went un-arrested? It is obviously erroneous to conclude that no arrest and no report of further criminal acts, imply that criminals have been deterred by their first arrests or imprisonment and consequently no crimes have been committed. Since it is difficult to objectively get the exact statistics of crimes actually committed and follow up their processes through arraignment and sentencing to the completion of prison terms, it is even more difficult to determine the effectiveness of crime deterrence. The study of deterrence takes us back to the very important question. What actually are the causes of crimes?

Science has proved that the best approach in solving a problem starts with tracing its root cause. Once the root cause is traced, finding the solution may become simple. While the effectiveness of crime deterrence is controversial, the numerous theories on the causes of crime on the other hand, simply remain mere speculations. Natural science speculates on genetic[42] and biological correlations; social sciences point to the environment and individual state of mind as possible causes. Economists in turn, relate them to the rational choice theory and the insatiable human wants and scarcity of means to meet these wants. All these research findings hopefully, might help in the formulation of long-term crime prevention policies.

---

[42]   James Q. Wilson and Joan Petersilia: <u>Crime: Public policies for Crime control</u>, CS Press Oakland CA.

f. Police Methods and Crime Deterrence

The traditional mission of law enforcement (the police, corrections, and related agencies) has been to enforce criminal law, whose main objective is crime deterrence or prevention. This is achievable through physical presence, patrol, arrest, detention, and investigation. People generally believe that the mere presence of a police officer at a particular location in our city or town, inspires some degree of security while at the same time produces a deterrent effect on potential offenders at that location. This may be true depending on the offender and how long the effect lasts. For instance, the presence of a police officer in the premises of a shopping center may dissuade an occasional or opportunistic bandit or robber, but not a hardened or professional bandit who would normally plan a counterstrategy to outwit the police officer or change the venue of his act.

The career criminal is a very intelligent fellow, often quite knowledgeable of his society's laws. He knows and is certain about the sanction reserved for whatever act he commits. He often rationalizes well on the costs and benefits of his actions and rapidly makes a conscious choice before engaging in a criminal act. From the criminal law perspective, effective deterrence presupposes awareness of a sanction by the violator of a social rule and the certainty of the sanction. The violator consciously weighs the cost and benefits of violating the social rule and decides for himself the best course of action. Fortunately or unfortunately, not all criminals are careerists.

Quoting Lafave (1965), Manning states that the original concept of arrest was to ensure the offender's appearance for judicial proceedings. But it has evolved to include the notion of punishment and revenge using legal means rather than self-help. Manning states further that the police has a different view of arrest. They do not view arrest as a means of deterrence but rather as a way of control, shamming, asserting their authority, shielding themselves from public criticism, and ensuring compliance with their commands. Referring to the case of Buzawa and Buzawa (1991), Manning contends that one cannot extrapolate the effectiveness of deterrence by basing one's judgment on reported cases of domestic violence because a vast majority of the cases are never reported to the police in the first place.

Police arrest or detention carried out with bias of any sort cannot produce a deterrent effect. When a police officer apprehends two offenders of different races (for instance, a black and a white person) and lets one person go while detaining the other on racial preference rather than on the basis of criminal guilt, this constitutes bias. Manifest bias often produces antisocial feelings of anger and revenge. This in turn, may nurture criminal intents in the mind of the victim of the act of bias. In the case of an open discriminatory arrest, no deterrent effect can be produced or achieved.

In his article on "Permeation of Race, National Origin and Gender Issues . . . ," Arthur Burnett[43] exposes injustice perpetuated by the police in their use of discreet power of arrest. He questions, what remedy other than revenge and further crimes can this state of affair produce? This is one of the several difficulties in evaluating the effectiveness of deterrence based on arrest rate. When the police let go a real offender on racial preference while arresting another one because of racial profiling/discrimination, the deterrent effect of the arrest is transformed into vengeance.

In a similar manner, a continuous crackdown on criminals by way of arrest and conviction only produces a counter effect of deterrence. Samuel Walker's[44] concept of "Get Tough: The Conservative Attack on Crime" contends that deterrence often loses its value when it becomes a common practice. He draws an analogy with the very high number of black American males in prison as a result of the intense crackdown on drug-related crimes and violence. In spite of this crackdown, crime continues to grow, and more people are arrested and imprisoned.

The public in general wants to see more police officers patrolling the streets as a measure of crime deterrence. Public security and safety are of course, sectors that governments hardly ignore. The US government invests annually a lot of money in national security as reflected in the statistics below. Police budgetary allocation experienced an increase from $20 billion to $100 billion (420 percent), while that of Corrections rose from $10 billion to $68 billon (660 percent), and that of the judicial rose from $10 billion to $47 billon (503 percent) between 1982 and 2006 respectively. There is no doubt that these departmental budget increases were used principally to recruit, train, and increase the number of personnel as well as logistics. The question however is this: Can an increase in the number of police officers alone really deter crimes? First of all, this option appears rather difficult to achieve for several reasons. The first practical difficulty is to have enough police officers to place everywhere in the cities. To achieve this objective implies that everyone would become a police officer. This of course, is impossible. The next problem is that of commitment. Having many officers everywhere is not having them conscientiously committed to their job. Another problem is that of resources/funding. Is it sensible and practically possible to commit all the nation's financial resources to law enforcement alone to fight crimes while abandoning other sectors like education, health, defense, and so forth? No political leader worth his name would do this.

---

43   Arthur Burnett, <u>American Criminal Law Review</u>, summer 1994 v31.
44   Samuel walker. <u>Sense and Non-sense about Crime and Drug</u>, 2001 Wadsworth.

Based on the statistics explained in the preceding paragraph obtained from the Bureau of Justice Statistics, we observe that since 1982, direct expenditure for each of the major criminal justice functions had experienced a steady increase (fig. 33 below). In spite of this heavy investment to fight crimes, we notice unfortunately a similarly steady increase rate in incarceration across the same period (fig. 34 below). This chart shows the number of offenders convicted and incarcerated under state and federal jurisdiction per 100,000 between1980 and 2002. Incarceration is a corollary of lawbreaking (crime), since people are arrested, convicted, and incarcerated for breaking the law. This increase in the incarceration rate could mean that with many police officers in the streets, more crimes than before were intercepted and more suspects than before were arrested and eventually tried, convicted, and incarcerated. Unfortunately, an increase in the number of law enforcement officers does not necessarily produce any deterrent effect on criminality. More officers in the streets might have helped to pick up more criminals whose crimes passed undetected when the officers were fewer.

Fig. 33 EXPENDITURE AND EMPLOYMENT EXTRACTS OF
CRIMINAL JUSTICE SERVICES FROM 1982 TO 1998

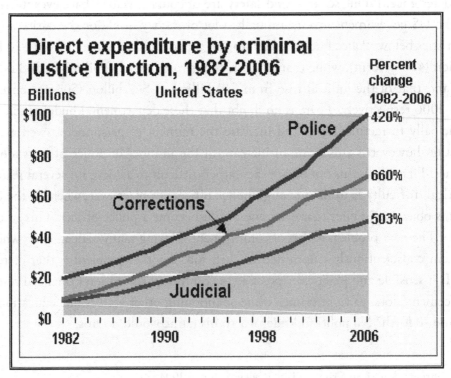

(Source: Bureau of Justice Statistics)

Fig. 34 US INCARCERATION RATE, 1980-2002

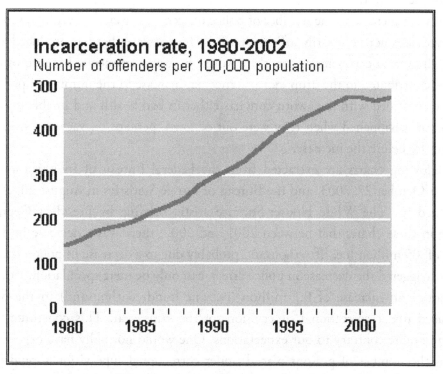

Incarceration rate, 1980-2002
Number of offenders per 100,000 population

(Source: Bureau of Justice Statistics)

In fact, several other difficulties abound attempting to achieve crime deterrence. Police crackdowns on criminals with numerous arrests and detentions have never dissuaded sworn criminals from their acts. Public policies in favor of police crackdowns as a crime deterrence measure, have often backfired in a chain reaction creating a series of social problems namely: overcrowded jails and corrections centers, budgetary increases, and pretrial case dismissals followed by a series of re-arrests.

The cases of Cincinnati and Sacramento County in California[45] are good examples of how serious crackdowns on drunk driving only create more difficult problems for the state and the criminal justice system. The result in the examples above was an increase in cases, increased need for judges, increased need for more jail space and facilities—all entailing an enormous financial cost for the state. The result is often a relapse in the law and release of offenders. This creates negative impressions in the mind of the offenders. They feel that the police was after all

---

[45]   Samuel walker. Sense and Non Sense about crime and Drugs, Wadsworth, 2001, page 113

wrong in making the arrest. This judicial backlash may plunge some offenders into revenge or reprisals for their arrest.

Similarly, an increase in the number of police officers in the city streets followed by a drop in crime rate does not necessarily affirm that it is this increase that has produced a deterrent effect. To draw a safe conclusion on this, would be quite erroneous because other factors might have contributed to the drop. For instance, an increase in the number of police officers might have coincided with the sworn convicts either in bad health and unable to operate for some time, or it happened when they were out of town, perhaps on vacation, or had moved somewhere else before the increase.

The following charts are extracted from the Federal Bureau of Investigation statistics compiled in October 27, 2003, and the Bureau of Justice Statistics in August 20, 2003. They are contained in "The White House: Social Statistic Briefing by President George Bush." We notice in these charts that between 2001 and 2002, there was a decrease in drug abuse violations of .05 million (i.e. fifty thousand probably due to a decrease in police arrests. What might have triggered the decrease in police arrest, can only be mere speculation. Paradoxically, we also notice an increase of 0.1 million (i.e. one hundred thousand) in the number of people placed under correctional supervision for the same year. This constitutes a curious phenomenon quite contrary to our expectations. One would normally have expected that an increase in the number of persons placed under correctional supervision should have been motivated by a corresponding increase in the arrest for drug abuse violations. The contrary seem to be the case. It is also mere speculations on what factors motivated the increase in the correctional population.

Several extrapolations can possibly be advanced for the reduced number of police arrests for drug-abuse violations during that period. Could the decrease in the number of drug-abuse violations have been triggered by the deterrent effect produced by the increase in incarceration rate for this offense? It might not necessarily have been so because other possible explanations abound. Either fewer people than before engaged in drug use that year or the police could not detect all the violators or drug supply sources were effectively blocked. There is no clear indication as to whether the reduced number of drug-abuse violations was motivated by any measure of deterrence or any crime prevention strategy. Whatever the case, it is implied that the increased number of placements under correctional supervision was proof of an increase in the number of drug offenders. This situation only further compounds and complicates the difficulty or controversy involving measurement of crime deterrence.

Table 4 COMPARATIVE CHARTS OF VIOLATION ARRESTS AND CORRECTIONAL POPULATIONS

Chart: **Arrests for Drug Abuse Violations.**	**Arrests for Drug Abuse Violations**	**Previous** 1.59 2001(in millions)	**Current** 1.54 2002 (in millions)
	The estimated number of arrests for drug abuse violations decreased slightly from 2001 to 2002.		
	Provided by Federal Bureau of Investigation as of October 27, 2003		
Chart: **National Correctional Populations**	**National Correctional Populations**	**Previous** 6.6 2001 (in Millions)	**Current** 6.7 2002 (in Millions)
	The number of people under correctional supervision increased 2.3% from 2001 to 2002.		
	Provided by Bureau of Justice Statistics as of August 20, 2003		

(Source: FBI and BJS)

g. Drunk Driving and Deterrence

While economists tend to believe in the effectiveness of deterrence, criminologists and sociologists continue to nurse steady skepticism. But recent economic studies on the effectiveness of deterrent policies on drunk driving seem to prove just the opposite of this assertion. It concludes that an increase in punishment is ineffective as a means of deterring driving under influence (DUI).

Bruce L. Benson, Brent D. Mast, and David W. Rasmussen,[46] refer to an empirical test of DUI deterrence performed by Wilkinson (1987) from 1976 to1980. In his study in which he

---

[46]   Bruce L. Benson, et al; <u>Applied Economics</u>, Feb 20, 2000 v32 i3 p357, "Can police deter drunk driving?"

(Wilkinson) used numerous variables to compare the differences in law enforcement efforts, he found that drunk-driving deterrent policies had no effect on the demand for alcohol. In another study, Cook (1980) observed that when the chances of detection or arrest are so minimal, there is no deterrent effect. He contends in conclusion that increase in alcohol tax and age-limit laws on the purchase and consumption of alcohol were better deterrent policy options against drunk driving than law enforcement crackdown methods. This conclusion remained spurious in my opinion because not every purchaser of alcoholic drinks may be a driver. Why then should those that do not drive at all be taxed? Besides, it is difficult for the seller of alcoholic drinks to determine who the purchaser at one particular moment is (a potential driver or not) and whether the alcoholic drink would be consumed before or after driving and also what amount of the drinks bought would be consumed before driving.

h. Public Expectations

After a violent criminal act, the public generally is angered. They expect to see the offender immediately arrested, tried, and punished for his crime. The public wants to see the offender kept under control away from the community of law-abiding citizens. They hope to be safe in the absence of the offender. The public perceives that immediate and severe punishment deters crimes. Amazingly, no sooner is a violent offender thrown into jail than another is born in the community. What actually explains this? Never in advance can we tell which of the faces we meet and talk to daily is hiding the criminal intent, until that masked face strikes down a victim. Then in fear and bewilderment we cry out for a more severe punishment again as if the first one was not severe enough to deter the crime. Unfortunately, even the death penalty does not seem to deter criminals.

Believing of course erroneously that crime prevention or deterrence is the sole province and responsibility of the criminal justice system, the public is ever quick to put the blame of rising crime rate to police inefficiency, lagging judicial processes, and ineffective correction programs. The police are blamed for slow responses to ongoing criminal activities and failure to make timely arrests and investigations. The police are also blamed for biased arrests motivated by racial profiling of offenders.

The public blame prosecutors and the court judges for unnecessary delays in trial and passing judgments. They are also blamed for what the public consider whimsical dismissal of cases, plea bargaining, or inadequate punishment for serious offenses. The correction department in turn, is blamed for poor conception and misapplication of programs that fail to meet expected reformatory and rehabilitation requirements. All these weaknesses the public believe, kill deterrence.

The unfortunate consequence of all these weaknesses is that, the wrong people are sometimes arrested, detained, and imprisoned while the real criminals go about scot-free in the community, committing more crimes. While those whose cases are out-rightly dismissed are speedily getting back to the community, others that receive very short prison sentences and inadequate reformation also quickly return to the community. Some of these fellows on return do resort either to revenge or fall back to new crimes. The public believe that law enforcement officers (police, the sheriff, and so forth) are well trained and armed enough to be up to their task. They are expected to be able to nip crimes in the bud. The courts should mete out very severe punishment to offenders (i.e. long sentences for violent crime offenders). But the question as to how long a prison term should be in order to produce the required deterrent effect remains a controversy.

The correction department, like the other actors on the criminal justice chain, is expected to adequately play its own role by applying the type of discipline, reformation, and rehabilitation that would deter offenders from further crimes even on release from prison. This is public expectation of crime deterrence. No reflection whatsoever is given to all the intricate mechanisms that involve the police profession, judicial procedures/processes, and adjudication of cases, let alone corrections' difficult task of keeping and controlling human beings behind the bars. When the crime rate goes high, the public feels that the criminal justice system has failed in crime deterrence. Expectations for immediate improvement become very high.

i. Public Health Perspective of Deterrence

Public health[47] perceives crime deterrence from the perspective of an infectious disease and prevention. It draws an analogy between disease and crime, distinguishing crime treatment from crime prevention. Prevention is a pre-intervention process aimed at stopping the invasion of the subject by the pathogen—in this case, crime. Meanwhile, treatment is a post-invasion process often more difficult to handle and complete successfully.

While prevention targets the risk factors that predispose to criminality, treatment aims at providing remedy to the offender. Remedy aims at eradicating the disease already within the subject. Treatment is always more expensive and difficult to manage because it requires

---

[47]   James Q. Wilson and Joan Petersilia; <u>Crime: Public policies for Crime control</u>, CS Press Oakland CA.

deployment of enormous resources and skill to minimize and stop the harm already done on the subject. A disease requires three favorable components to occur namely: the pathogen, the environment, and a susceptible host. In a similar manner, any crime requires the offender, a favorable environment, and the target/victim to occur.

Consequently, the absence of any one of these components automatically prevents the occurrence of the crime. Further in this analogy, public health clearly stands for prevention (deterrence) as a better approach to solving criminality. Altering one of the three criminal components may help in crime deterrence. Some public health professionals recommend long-term treatment programs (e.g. mental health treatment for criminals with histories of related illnesses or other causes) as alternative to punishment.

PART VIII

A. COMMUNITY CRIME-PREVENTION PROGRAMS

I n the course of our studies, we have realized that neither increases in police presence and arrest, certainty and severity of sanctions, death penalty, or any form of severe punishment of criminals have been found to produce any substantial degree of deterrence on prospective criminals. Implicitly, the work of the entire criminal justice system is thus put to question. Where then do we go from here? The seemingly reasonable alternative to deterrence is long-term crime prevention strategies.

a. Continuous Training and Supervision

Firstly, long-term prevention policies for youths and infants that include continuous training and supervision both in and out of school contexts seem to produce some positive results. Fortunately, most of what I am suggesting here is already in practice in most communities, though not everywhere.

b. Isolation into High-Security Facilities

Secondly, incapacitating career and most violent criminals is another way of remedying the situation. This means isolating and placing hardened criminals that can no longer respond to reform and rehabilitation efforts in high-security facilities away from the community for life. The next approach involves providing correction and rehabilitation programs for criminals judged to be opportunists or mentally deficient. Then we place at-risk youths at early stages in their lives in well-supervised residential training programs so as to protect them and decrease in them the likelihood of committing crimes. Mixing youths in the same correction facilities where adult convicts are held, is not a good idea because their close proximity to hardened adult convicts only helps in their destruction, since they will always interact with these adult convicts and pick up some of their bad habits. A completely separate facility is a better option if correction departments hope to succeed in their reformation and rehabilitation programs.

c. Supervised Residential Training Programs

Fortunately, this is what the juvenile justice system is already doing in the United States. The most lauded effort in this area is the Massachusetts Department of Youth Services[48] that has become a model emulated by other states such as Maryland, Florida, and Utah, to name just a few. In the state of Massachusetts, an initiative shifting the former state-operated training programs to community-based ones yielded great fruits as evidenced by post-reform lower recidivism rate among the youths. Working with a reduced number of youths in community-based contexts has proven to be more productive than in state-run juvenile institutions. Attacking juvenile criminality seems to be of utmost importance because most adult criminals we have today, developed their skills as they grew up in crimes settings or crime-prone environments.

d. Supervised After-School Programs

When we alter individual susceptibility to crimes by taking away those factors that predispose the subject to criminality, we theoretically deter crime commission. Instead of waiting for an unsupervised or idle youth to commit a crime and we the parents or school authorities call the police on him or start thinking of occupying him after school, it would be better to start organizing supervised after-school programs like sports competitions, scouting,

---

[48] 1. Peter W. Greenwood. "Juvenile Crime and Juvenile Justice"
2. James Q. Wilson and Joan Petersilia: <u>Crime: Public policies for Crime control</u>, CS Press Oakland CA.

gardening, animal breeding, or theater art performances to occupy the youths. It is commonly said that "an idle mind is the devil's den." Social opportunities are good alternatives that can occupy at-risk juveniles and prevent them from falling into the ready hands of voracious adult drug dealers or criminals always lurking within the communities, looking for easy preys to recruit into their criminal or drug team.

Medical treatment and sanctions or punishment have independently proved unfruitful in preventing or deterring juvenile criminality. Strategies or public policies that aimed at taking away those factors that predispose youths or at-risk children to criminal activities are deterrent in nature, and should be implemented in areas where juvenile delinquency is becoming a cause for concern.

e. Altering Environment or "Hot Spots"

The success of programs that keep children away from crimes is irrefutable, although the cost remains very high and discouraging. Other community-based strategies that aim at altering the environment or places or "hot spots" predisposing youth to criminal activities, consist of renovating and putting into use abandoned houses. If not possible, out-rightly clearing them away is recommended. Another important approach is limiting unmonitored youth gatherings. Youths have the tendency of hanging out idly in bands or groups in market squares or popular social sports especially in late hours of the day extending late into the nights. And it is during such encounters that antisocial or deviant habits are exhibited by already experienced ones and also emulated by new ones. It is during such encounters that drug addicts recruit new members for initiation into their groups. Law enforcement officers must take note of this and constantly patrol these areas while monitoring keenly their activities.

f. Employing Social Counselors

Other strategies include modifying or altering those stages in the development of youths that reveal delinquent tendencies like unruliness, aggressiveness, and lack of self-control. Parents can address these aspects individually at home or by using the services of specially trained social counselors in residential placement training programs or those offered by school authorities where the cases are not yet a major cause for concern. Such efforts doubtlessly will contribute enormously in the realization of a long-term criminal deterrence policy. The downside of all this is no doubt, the great financial implications to the state. In spite of the high cost, it is better for a nation to have a sane and healthy youth population than that made up of criminals.

Asserting that traditional criminal justice methods of police crackdowns, arrest, detention, trial, and punishment in the form of long prison sentences or even death penalties have not so far effectively produced significant crime deterrence is hardly an overstatement. In fact, all evidence points to this fact. Criminologists, social scientists, and other scholars concerned with the scientific study of crime unfortunately still remain speculative in their theories and modalities as to the evaluation of crime deterrence. They however, do agree on one point: alternative training programs that everything being equal may produce better long-term crime deterrence.

Indeed, reference needs to be made to those programs that either incapacitate or reform and rehabilitate career or opportunistic criminals respectively. Any modern technological tool applicable in this area of studies may be built on these main concepts for the attainment of better results. Punishment as guarantor of crime deterrence has evidently failed to yield any significant fruits and may be conveniently discarded for once in favor of treatment-oriented policies.

B. TREATMENT PROGRAMS: CASE STUDY

Understanding how some of the treatment programs work and how they impact the subject placed in the program is very important in our overall assessment of the program. The program we are going to study is a residential supervised probation. It is a true-to-life story of two young girls committed to a residential probation program following their convictions for crimes they actually committed. The following factors surrounding these two cases that should be of great interest to us based on our subject matter are the subjects' backgrounds, their socioeconomic conditions, their environments, their lifestyles, their families, and social strains that they go through. All these factors potentially at the origin of their crimes, exert a lot of influence in the treatment programs that they are subjected to. In fact, a movie entitled *Growing Up on the Inside* had been produced based on their true stories by Liz Garbus. Two main characters are involved in Garbus's film: Megan and Shannae. They both belong to a low socioeconomic class. Megan is a white young girl from a single parent. Her mother (Vanessa), a wayward drug addict, is imprisoned for four years in Baltimore city Detention

Center, Maryland. Abandoned thus and living with foster parents, Megan gets out of hand and falls into a street gang and drugs at sixteen years of age. She gets involved in an assault. She is arrested and committed to the Waxler Juvenile Facility in Maryland by the court. After doing some time there, she is assessed and recommended for probation by the treatment team and the administration of the center. During her evaluation interview, she is very evasive and manifests a nonchalant attitude towards her family. She does not bother about her mother; rather she wants her father who unfortunately, she has never known. Her nonchalance is justified since she had not really experienced or had known the importance of maternal or paternal love and warmth.

The court grants her probation on certain conditions. She is very excited about leaving the prison and to live a free life again. She is assigned to an apartment in the heart of the city under the supervision of a case manager provided by the State of Maryland Juvenile Justice System. Poorly supervised and without a job or any source of income, Megan starts violating the terms of her probation. She resumes hanging out, this time with her cousin and other street-gang friends with whom they smoke and use drugs.

A visit to her mother in prison only reveals the deep social rift that exists between the two of them. On her release from prison, her mother like Megan, cannot adjust to normal social life. Her treatment in prison was ineffective. Mother and daughter cannot cohabit smoothly. Megan would not heed her mother's advice to refrain from street life. She strongly challenges her mother and openly defies her with insults. As Vanessa tries to solicit her own mother's advice, her mother throws the blame back on her, and both end up in disagreement. It is amazing to note that Vanessa's mother had lived the same lifestyle. We notice an interesting irony here. Megan blames all her weaknesses on her mother (Vanessa), just as Vanessa blames all hers on her own mother (i.e. Megan's grandmother).

Each one disagrees with the other's lifestyle even though she is living the same lifestyle. Apparently blinded by their drug conditions, they become so pessimistic and only tend to look backward at each other with blame rather than forward. They all seem to be living in a dream, while life sleeps away with them. Already deeply influenced by their addiction, they cannot make a conscious and sane decision for themselves. The sequel of this disagreement is definite separation. Vanessa bewildered, abandons Megan in the car in the street and walks away forever back to prison through another crime. Each one digs deeper into her lifestyle and doom. Megan continues with her gang life, and her poor grandmother and mother are left behind in pathetic solitude to psychologically nurse their life failure as they see their progeny sink into depravity.

Shannae is a young black girl of the African American minority group. She is about sixteen years old and comes from a low-income single-family background. She grows up alone with her mother, and at the age of eleven she was sexually abused (raped). Neither she nor her mother portrays any drug-related past history. While in school, she stabbed a friend to death in the course of a fight and was sentenced to three years' imprisonment in the Waxler Juvenile Facility in Maryland. There she meets Megan. She seems to conform well to therapy, and after assessment by the team of therapists and the center's administration, she is approved for probation.

The courts grant it, and she is assigned to the Florence Gritter Group Home. She is happy to leave prison and is picked up by her mother to this group home where she adjusts very quickly to a new life. Two weeks later, her mother dies. She struggles to get a job and continues with her education. She however, picks up well academically and graduates high school in pomp and encouragement from her extended family members and her distant father. From there she moves on to college. Without necessarily ruling out other possible causes, it is obvious that the crimes of these two girls were theoretically motivated by strain. If we should objectively buy Quinney's concept that **"what is important in the study of crime is everything that happens before crimes . . . Crime is a reflection of something larger and deeper"** (Chesley-Lind)[49], then it would be important to examine their socioeconomic environments, past lives, and experiences before making any pronouncement about them. Both girls belong to a low-income minority social stratum.

Single-family structures cannot provide adequate parenting or generate enough income to sustain the family. Their low-income conditions might have pushed Megan's mother into drug sale as a means of earning some additional income to support herself and her daughter. In doing so, she socially isolated herself from her daughter. The paradox here is that she eventually dragged her daughter along into the same game. Lacking the fatherly presence and warmth that would have filled the isolation created by her mother's aloofness, Megan went to the street apparently to fill this social vacuum. In doing so, she only ends up in the same condition like her mother. Shannae at her early age, lost her virginity through sexual abuse. This might have emotionally affected her perspective of life. Sexual abuse can induce what Agnew has termed in his strain theory "actual or anticipated presentation of negative

---

49   Chesney-Lind and Pasko, 2004 chapter 14, p210, <u>Girls, Women, and Crimes</u>, SAGE Publications, Thousand Oaks, London.

or noxious stimuli."[50] All these conditions Agnew contends, account for strain that pushes subjects to become deviant or to engage in criminal activities.

Social scientists contend that since criminal justice systems are unable to develop appropriate crime control strategy from its causal perspective, the only apparent remedy left is to resort to treatment, rehabilitation, and reintegration. Social reintegration is an arduous process that involves preparation of the convicted person for a smooth regain and resumption of post-penal life. A number of factors including the subject's willing participation, are involved. Firstly, the prison environment including all the participants such as the staff, the administering authorities, social workers, therapists, have an important part to play in this process. Secondly, the society, family, community, and the state where the person has to return to after his/her stay in prison also have a stake in the process. Thirdly, the subject's willingness to change is very important in the whole process.

The subjects themselves have to open up and show a conscious willingness to embrace the change. Once this is absent like in the case of Megan, all efforts made are doomed to fail. Megan's responses during the evaluation interview are not only evasive but passive and playful. She reveals no element of seriousness or conscious concern about her therapy, let alone her reformation process. What we read on the faces of the members of the treatment team is frustration and disappointment motivated by Megan's elusive responses to their questions. Judging from their impressions during the interview, one could rightly conclude that she would not be granted probation. But shockingly, she so easily got it. Whether it was the fault of the court or that of the treatment team we cannot state with certainty. This however, constitutes a weakness on the criminal justice system. Her placement in the heart of the city in very close proximity to the very type of activities that took her away from a conventional lifestyle in the first place is another weakness on the part of the Maryland Juvenile Justice System.

Her case manager shares the blame in her reversion to her past lifestyle. The case manager fails to take appropriate measures to revoke her probation when she started violating it. Indeed her lifestyle a year later only proved that she did not deserve probation, let alone ready for it. Though her subsequent failure in social reintegration may partly be blamed variously on all these factors mentioned above including even her family that she does not have, the greater blame is hers. She is rational, calculative, and deliberate in her actions (Samenow 1984). She is very arrogant and insulting to her mother, on whom she blames all her faults. Her refusal to make any effort to follow her probation rules or to heed her mother's advice indicates that her

---

[50]   Cullen, Ball and al,2002, page 60. <u>Criminological Theory</u>, SAGE Presentation, Thousand Oaks, London.

crime is in her mind and she knows what she is doing. "Crime resides in the minds of human being and is not caused by social conditions" (Samenow).[51] Meanwhile, Shannae having gone through a similar strain (except perhaps for the drug she might never have taken before), learned to adjust and eventually gained social reintegration much easily. She is conscious of her offense, expresses remorse for it, and willingly opens her heart to her therapy in the center. We could read this acknowledgement in the minds of the members of the treatment team. She merits her probation, which came readily, and she made proper use of it in the group home. In spite of the shock caused by her mother's sudden death and related strains, she is optimistic and pushes forward in life. She welcomes even her distant father and reshapes her life. This conscious effort and willingness to embrace the change earns her easy reintegration and acceptance in her community.

Community's contribution in helping these girls in their reintegration efforts could be material support with school needs, provision of free boarding, and jobs. It could also be through institution of antidrug counseling programs, after-school activities, or programs that would involve and keep them away from deviant groups or associations.

Imprisonment irrespective of motive is social ostracism. It infantilizes even the most responsible of persons. It renders the convict irresponsible because one is deprived of one's civic rights and power of decision. As if this social isolation is not enough, the convict is again subjected to the whims of the authorities and staff of the institution. Imprisonment deprives the convict even of the right to break his/her window and save himself/herself from a cell on fire. This depressing effect of imprisonment is made heavier on women than men by virtue of their gender and social responsibilities over the family. Unlike men, women are by nature the bearers and carriers of the offspring. It is their natural duty to ensure the proper nurturing of children. Their natural condition as the weaker sex and responsibility put the woman in a prejudiced position when it concerns transgressing social constructs (laws).

The case of a single parent (mother only) makes the situation even worse. Once imprisoned, the woman undergoes more emotional strain than a man. Pointless to state that everyone's sympathy naturally goes to a convicted nursing mother than to another person involved in the same offense and penalty. Imprisonment renders the convicted mother irresponsible because she is deprived of the care and warmth she naturally owes her children. What are the needs of a woman on leaving prison after serving a sentence? Before examining

---

[51]   Samenow, 1984. Inside the Criminal Mind, Times Books, New York

these needs, let us like Quinney (2002),[52] first of all look briefly at the type of women that go to prison, what their crimes are, their ethnic distribution, and their social backgrounds prior to imprisonment.

Studies have shown that majority of the women incarcerated in US prisons are ethnically blacks, Hispanic, and non-white (Chesney-Lind and Pasko 2004).[53] They are mostly single parents with children less than eighteen years. They are involved in nonviolent drug-related and property offenses. Majority of them earlier in age and before imprisonment had suffered from some sort of abuse such as sexual (rape) and domestic violence. They have been victims of different forms of discrimination—racial, job opportunities and training, legal suits, and unfair criminal justice administration—leaving them with a single family, helpless, and poor. The lifestyles imposed on them by their social status prior to imprisonment already transforms some of them into patients of depression or other forms of psychosis, HIV, STD, or alcoholism. This explains why most of them on incarceration are usually committed to different types of psychiatric treatment, alcoholism, drug, or a sort of parenting skill, and job training programs. How effective are these treatment programs before their release from prison? This is the question.

The needs of a woman leaving the prison are centered on the above causes of their imprisonment. For better discussion, it will be necessary if we sum them up fairly into three main topics: neighborhood conditions, community resources, and public policies.

Even the most normal of persons once imprisoned usually experiences some degree of psychological trauma that automatically transforms the person into a patient. A woman leaving prison is a patient, at least psychologically. She is going out to face a social stigma and distrust from her neighborhood imposed on her by her imprisonment. The humiliation that comes with having been to prison is an inhibiting factor to her effort to reestablish social links with her children, her family, and her community residents at large. **"Do you know what it is like to try to get through the day with an X on your back (a criminal record)? People don't want to hire you, no one want to rent you apartment, you can't count on your family because they have given up on you, your church calls you a sinner and no one trusts you"** (Chesley-Lind and Pasko, 240).

She is above all, faced with compounding demands. She needs a residence in order to get back custody of what is left of her children. Getting a residence is contingent upon getting a

---

[52]   Quinney (2002) contends that what is important in the study of crime is everything that happens before a crime occurs. That crime is a reflection of something larger and deeper.

[53]   Chesney-Lind and Pasko, 2004. Girls, Women, and Crime. SAGE Publications. Thousand Oaks.

job that will enable her to pay the rents and related utilities. Getting a job requires that she has recovered well from her strained condition or drug addiction so as to be able to withstand work-related pressures. If at all she can prove this, her credential already has a stigma, and few employers would be willing to give her a job. For how long can a generous extended family member take care of her and her children? Long separation due to imprisonment has strained this relationship. Reestablishing relationships with her children, her family, and her community is an ordeal.

The life in a correction facility is characterized by a military-type discipline that is alien to a normal woman's nature. This in itself constitutes an important source of strain. Once adjusted to this prison lifestyle, readjusting to the rhythm of conventional society that she had almost forgotten during her imprisonment is a new source of strain on her.

Treatment programs commenced in prison are hardly ever effective due either to insufficiency, inconsistency, or other administrative constraints. Thus on release, she needs to continue with them. Here is the grief of one of the patients Beth Richie,[54] interviewed: "I really need help, but didn't get it in jail. So when I came out, I went right back (to drug abuse). Nothing has changed." Continuing with her treatment programs, readjusting to society, going to work, and taking care of her children are stressful. She needs the skills required for the job she contemplates to do. Just like Vanessa, Megan's mother in Liz Garbus's film,[55] every parent would undergo more psychological trauma than before capable of deepening her involvement in crime, when she realizes on release from prison that her child has gone out of hand.

Explaining the effect of added strain on an already strained subject, Agnew[56] in his strain theory contends that "the higher the dose of strain that a person experiences, the greater the likelihood of the person being engaged in crime or in some form of deviance." The degree of strain that Vanessa and Megan experience on their release from imprisonment requires a special training, a high degree of commitment, and adequate community resources to handle. When their families and community failed to provide this, they were thrown back into crimes and eventual imprisonment. Besides material needs, a woman on release from prison also naturally needs to satisfy her natural emotions of love. She is returning to meet some of the very people who might have contributed to her plight. She is faced with the

---

[54] Beth Richie is the author of an article "Challenges Incarcerated Women Face As they Return To Their Communities" in <u>Girls, Women and Crimes</u> by Chesney-Lind and Pasko.

[55] Liz Garbus's film is adapted on *Girlhood: growing Up on the Inside*, the story of two young women convicted for violent crimes and committed by the criminal justice system in the state of Maryland to therapy in the Waxler Juvenile Facility.

[56] Cullen, Ball and al,2002, page 60. <u>Criminological Theory</u>, SAGE Presentation, Thousand Oaks, London.

problem of getting the right partner that would be blind to her past criminal life and return her love sincerely. She does not need a crook that would come into her life only to exploit, strain, and throw her back into prison. So faced with these problems, what the woman on release from prison needs first of all is the community and family connection to smoothen this dreadful transition. Community and family connection must be inspired by a humane and nonjudgmental approach in her reception back into society. Her reintegration back into society must be backed by a spirit of forgiveness and reconciliation rather than repulsion and distrust. All support whether material or moral, should spring from a foundation of genuine love that usually inspires forgiveness. If the society is not ready to love and forgive them, then their reintegration would be meaningless and unachievable. Besides material support that a community should provide her such as public funding, housing, medical care, some form of transportation, job training, and employment, the community should provide her with the moral support she needs for social readjustment.

To facilitate social reintegration, special treatment programs for women leaving prison should be planned and implemented well ahead of time. Special programs like drug addiction and alcohol treatment, parenting skill training, and job skill training to enable them to earn employments and keep jobs on eventual release are necessary. In order to ease the transition back to conventional life, visitation program for families should be established and encouraged among female convicts and their family members and children. For instance, programs like the Girl Scouts Beyond Bars in Ohio State, New Jersey, Missouri (Chesney-Lind and Pasko), would contribute a lot in their reintegration.

The criminal justice system has been under serious criticism for applying harsh punishment that recycles rather than deters crime. It is unjustifiable and absurd to punish a woman more severely than a man in a drug crime in which she was merely an innocent abettor. Fairness should be applied in rendering justice. When a woman is punished unjustly unlike the man, the effect of the punishment usually extends to the innocent children that the woman would abandon to do her heavy punishment. Do these innocent infants deserve such a fate? This is the moral question for those who apply such unfair justice.

When economic opportunities are not equitably distributed to all sectors of society irrespective of sex, race, and social strata that might have been established by the more powerful, when social and legal structures do not cease to encourage gender discrimination, and when criminal law and criminal justice are not applied impartially and swiftly so as to actually serve their purpose of deterrence, then crimes are bound to continue to rise, and the woman would always remain the pathetic victim of it all.

Since the development of perfect crime control measures is an illusion, it would be absurd to conclude that the above strategies, if implemented fully, would stop crime recycling among women. This assertion is similar to the contention that we cannot actually explain the causes of white-collar crimes with the strain theory. However, some of these measures hopefully may positively affect the recidivism rate, though a good number of female criminals may still become recidivists in some other crimes.

PART IX

STALKING: A LESS RECOGNIZED FORM OF CRIME

Stalking is another form of crime that is hardly noticed or recognized as such by some criminal justice systems. A report[57] on a study by Fisher, Cullen, and Turner conducted at a national level in 1997 on stalking victimization among college women in the United States revealed the following information. Each one of us after reading may decide whether stalking should be considered criminal or not. A survey of college women was conducted over a period of seven months on stalking incidence. At the end of the study, 31.1 percent of the women reported that they had been stalked for periods that typically lasted two months. Even though the incidents involved frequent contacts with the offenders often prompting them to seek for protection, the women reported no incident of physical harm perpetuated on them. The study typically revealed a strong correlation between the risk of victimization and the women's lifestyle routine activities, prior sexual victimization, and demographic characteristics. Women between the ages of eighteen to twenty-nine were the main targets. Before delving into the report, let us attempt to understand what stalking actually means.

---

[57]   The report was published in <u>Criminology and Public Policy</u>. Columbus: March 2002 vol.1.

a. Definition and Theoretical Consideration

To stalk[58] (verb) variously means "to pursue a game or person stealthily." Indeed, to pursue or approach a subject stealthily in order to prey on. Stalking as implied in the above definition, portrays an evil intention on the part of the perpetrator. In general, the concept of stalking involves willful, malicious, and repeated pursuing, harassing, or threatening another person (Tjaden and Thoennes 1998).[59] It also includes lying in wait for and surveillance, as well as nonconsensual communication, and vandalism of property belonging to the subject.

Although in the United States, states and federal legislations differ in their definitions of stalking, it is however agreed that engaging repeatedly in a harassing or threatening behavior towards another person—such as appearing at the person's home or place of business without any express reason; making repeated calls verbally or by phone; sending or leaving e-mails, written messages, or objects at the person's home or place of work; and vandalizing the person's property in order to attract his or her attention—all amount to stalking and are hence offensive and criminal.

These acts in themselves may or may not amount to assault or murder. While some states would want to qualify stalking as a crime based on a quantitative ratio, others base their definition on the degree or credibility of the threat of harm ensuing from the act of stalking. Theoretically, stalking can be considered the outcome of a lifestyle routine activity characterized by four factors namely: physical proximity of victims to motivated offenders, placing subjects to risky or deviant situations, exposing subjects as targets to offenders, or isolating the subject from any form of guardianship.

Meanwhile, the stalker motivated by rational choice, may want to obtain something from the victim. Stalking does not occur by accident from someone under psychopathic influences or suffering from a psychotic fit. The offender consciously decides to respond to love pressures based on previous intimate relations or unreciprocated infatuation for a new acquaintance, to utilitarian desires, or simply to the desire to revenge some antecedents. He may perhaps be acting on self-interest or on hire to do evil.

---

[58] Webster's Encyclopedic unabridged Dictionary of the English Language.
[59] Tjaden and Thoennes in 1998 carried out a research on "Stalking in America: Findings from the National Violence against Women Survey" for the US Department of Justice.

It is amazing that until 1990 when anti-stalking laws were passed in California following the murder of the young actress Rebecca Schaeffer, no such legislation had existed before criminalizing the act of stalking. However, the National Victim Center and Survivors of Stalking in collaboration with the media, persistently aroused public awareness to this crime by continuously publicizing more stalking cases with fatal outcomes involving even public officials as well as Hollywood stars. This action eventually led to the criminalization of stalking by most legislatures across the nation. What is the degree of prevalence of stalking victimization? What are the different forms of stalking and impact on victims? Who are the victims of stalking and how do they cope with it? What are the risk factors for stalking? What are its policy implications? These are the questions that I will attempt to answer in the following pages.

b. Degree of Prevalence

It is of interest to note that our knowledge of the degree of prevalence, victim statistics, and risk factors of stalking remains very limited in spite of continuous media coverage and heightened awareness to this crime. The FBI and National Crime Victimization Survey (NCVS), incidentally does not collect statistics on stalking victims at national levels. Similarly, there are no state, local, or federal statistics on people arrested, prosecuted, or convicted on stalking charges.

Jeremy Travis[60] (1996), in support of this opinion contends that, this limitation can be explained by the fact that very little research had been undertaken in this area of public concern. He further regrets that this omission has unfortunately prevented the formulation of policies that would have helped in checking this phenomenon. However, a National Institute of Justice report of 1996 reveals about 20,000 to 200,000 numbers of stalkers in the United States, with an estimated 19.78 per 100,000 women eighteen years and older.

In another survey conducted in 1996 in post-secondary institutions based on a six-month period (Mustaine and Tewksbury 1999), 10.5 percent of the females sampled admitted having been stalked. Similarly, in two other surveys of undergraduate students of psychology in West Virginia University, an average of 30.9 percent of the females revealed having been stalked at least once. According to the results of US census estimates, one out of twelve women (8.2 million or 8 percent) and one out of forty-five men (2 million or 2 percent), have been stalked

---

[60]   Jeremy Travis was director of the National Institute of Justice in 1996.

at least once in their lifetime. Accordingly, an estimated 1,006,970 women and 370,990 men are stalked annually in the United States.

c. Forms of Stalking and Impact on Victims

The most common and devastating concerns faced by stalking victims are fear of violence and threat of life. Initial contact between the stalker and victim is not a precondition in the determination of the offense of stalking. Whether contact had existed before or not does not affect the crime of stalking. Stalking can take several forms. It could be direct, where the two are actually in close physical proximity, or indirect through visual, audio, or other forms of technological contact.

The stalker for instance, could have seen the victim's photo, heard the voice by phone, and corresponded with the victim by e-mail using the Internet or by postal service. A person can be stalked through any of these forms. Victims of stalking have been known to experience repeated pursuits and direct or indirect harassment by phone, resulting in fear and concern for their safety. Female victims have been known to change their life patterns in order to ward off potential stalkers. In fact, some female victims find themselves virtually imprisoned psychologically and living in the permanent fear of harm.

d. Victims of Stalking and Coping Strategies

Studies have proved that stalking is a gender-neutral crime. Both men and women have been victims of stalking. However, the ratio of women stalked as compared with that of men remains very high. For instance, it was revealed that 72 percent of those stalked were women and 22 percent were men. An overall comparison revealed that 87 percent of stalkers identified by victims were men (Tjaden and Thoennes 1998), and the remaining 13 percent were women. As to the motive behind stalking, victims perceived that they were stalked because the stalker wanted to instill fear or to get control of them. Sexual motivations were not utterly ruled out. Considering that stalking is motivated by sex passion, women doubtlessly become more victims of this crime than the men who are motivated offenders. The propensity for males to pursue the females for a sexual relationship even to the point of using force is more or less a banal affair, when we recall the hegemonic tendencies that are inherent in male nature. This is not to exclude the fact that men might have been stalked for sexual motives by women as revealed by the studies.

A deeper study of this survey by Tjaden and Thoennes shows annual estimates in which women's stalking rates were 2.5 times more than those of men (1.0 percent). The same report revealed that 52 percent of victims of stalking were women within the age range of eighteen to twenty-nine years old. Existing research also reveals that college students especially women, are more at risk of this type of sexual victimization than other categories of women. This research conclusion is logically significant for the reason that people between the ages of eighteen to twenty-nine, representing 71 percent of 4.6 million women (US Department of Education 1997), were mostly students enrolled in colleges. Coping strategies for victims who knew their stalkers have mostly been to ignore the stalkers, or to hang up on them if it was by phone. While some bold victims openly confronted and challenged the stalkers, others simply modified their schedules in order to avoid them completely. Other studies revealed that majority of the victims were reluctant to involve the police and the magistrate courts for fear of reprisals. For instance, in a survey of 512 women randomly selected in a southeast university, 24.7 percent of the female students admitted having been stalked at least once, and 23.8 percent responded having been threatened with physical violence. Two-thirds of the stalking was not reported to the police out of fear of reprisal.

e. Risk Factors Favorable to Stalking

Associated with stalking victimization are threats, substance abuse, and the absence of a psychotic disorder. Most stalking offenders are quite motivated and rational. Other strong correlates are prior intimate relationship between victim and offender and a history of violent behavior. Following an analysis of factors that increased the risk of stalking victimization based on ethnic determinants, Tjaden and Theonnes noted that stalking was more common for younger American Indian women and Alaskan natives and less for Asian women. This trend was to be admitted cautiously, as there was no clear indicator in their findings to explain the variance other than a small sampling population. Basing their studies on social domain, other explanations of risk factors associated with stalking were developed on a lifestyle-routine activity theory (Mustaine 1997 and Tewksbury 1999).

This theory states that a certain number of factors increased the risk of stalking. These factors are a lifestyle and living location that puts the subject in close physical proximity with the offender, exposure of the subject to a criminal environment where drugs are sold and used, presenting the subject as target to the offender, or placing the subject in situations where there is no guardianship to deter potential stalkers.

Those who live alone often lack the social guardianship that may deter potential stalkers. This is very possible when the stalker uses close contact such as physically following the subject, lying in wait, or indirect contact such as telephoning. It is easier for anyone whether former intimate or stranger, to stalk a person who lives alone because there will be no one to intervene to deter him. Proximity to motivated offenders also places the subject at the risk of stalking. Female students living in boarding houses or single apartments are at risk of stalking. Demographic characteristics such as ages between eighteen to twenty-nine years (of course, suitable age of college women), also contribute to stalking. Based on this theory, the risk of stalking would also be surely higher for individuals who engage in social or recreational activities that pull potential stalkers. For instance, campus life where students are often pulled together by social gatherings such as parties, musical concerts, sports competitions, fraternities, and club meetings provide good opportunities for stalking.

f. Legal and Policy Implications of Stalking

Even though the first anti-stalking law was passed in California in 1990, stalking had actually started receiving public attention in 1989. In 1992 the US Congress joined other states legislations by passing the anti-stalking law. This was in response to heightened media coverage of cases of murdered women resulting from reported stalking. The shooting to death in 1993 of Rebecca Schaeffer, a young actress, by an obsessed fan who had stalked her earlier, and the murder of the five women in Orange County by their former boyfriends who had also stalked them, aroused more public awareness to this crime than it had done before then. The lack of statistics on cases of stalking victimization led Fisher et. al.[61] in a seven-month national-level study of stalking among college women in 1997, to erect stalking to the rank of social problems that merit public policy intervention. The results of their research fortunately led to the Congress act that became a model for different states, that soon built their legislations on this legal framework. This act also gave birth in 1994 to the Violence Against Women Act (VAWA) title IV enclosed in Public Law number 103-322. Federal, state, and local courts all have since then been involved in the fight against stalking crimes. For instance, the Sixth US

---

[61] Fisher and al; Being Pursued: Stalking victimization in a national study of college women, <u>Criminology and Public Policy</u>. Columbus in March, 2002

Circuit Court of Appeals in a 1994 trial, ruled in favor of an Ohio state conviction of Jerry Lee Staley, a Michigan man convicted for a fifteen—to twenty-five-year prison sentence for stalking his ex-girlfriend in Barry County. The offender was accused of breaking into the victim's home, calling her up to fifteen times per day, chasing her with a baseball bat, and threatening to "slice her gut"[62] with a knife.

g. Methods Used in the Research

Fisher et al. developed and tested a number of hypotheses about the risk of being stalked based on the lifestyle routine activities of the subjects. They developed two forms of questionnaires: a stalking screen question, and an incident questionnaire based on the National Crime Victimization Survey. They used them to conduct a survey of 4,446 women of two years' and four years' college and university. Limiting their selection only to those institutions with 1,000 students, they made a random selection of 233 institutions: 39 two-year and 194 four-year schools from which they got a random selection of students. The students were mailed covered letter questionnaires and later on contacted by phone. Participation was voluntary.

They were provided a free phone number for verification of the legitimacy of the study if they expressed any doubt. The result revealed an 84.6 percent response rate based on the following feedback: 4,446 responded and 496 abstained out of a total of 5,769 contacted. In order to avoid possible bias that could be introduced by a broad definition of stalking, for instance, considering it a petty form of attention-seeking behavior characteristic of male students, the researchers used screen questions specifically qualifying stalking as repetitive, obsessive, and fear causing with possible bodily harm. More information was collected from respondents in order to actually classify the stalking as criminal or not. Similarly, the researchers also took appropriate measures not to commit the "opposite error", (Moynihan 1993)[63] by dismissing the stalking as irrelevant and not worth incriminating simply because the victim considered it not serious enough to report or call in the police.

---

[62]   By Dee-Ann Durbin/Associated Press. This quotation is drawn from the direct words of the stalker as reported by the victim during trial.

[63]   Moyniham (1993) calls "opposite error" or "defining deviance down" the normalization of unwanted male intrusion into women's lives.

h. Data Collection

Data collection was done by Schulman, Ronca & Bucuvalas, Inc. (SRBI) using a computer-aided telephone interviewing system (CATI). Telephone calls were made by professionally well-trained female interviewers for a period of two and a half months. Stalking was defined in conformity with state and federal level legal definitions (i.e. the act of repeatedly pursuing another with the intention of causing fear or bodily harm that made the person afraid or concerned about her safety). To determine the nature and extent of stalking, a questionnaire was developed to measure demographic characteristics of the respondent, including lifestyle at individual level. After determining the nature and extent of stalking, an incident level questionnaire was developed to gather information on the effects of stalking on the victim and measures taken. To perform a multivariate analysis measure, the researchers used the lifestyle routine theory to select the following variables: proximity to motivated offender, exposure to crime, attractiveness of target, availability of guardianship, prior victimization, and demographics.

i. Extent and Characteristics of Stalking

The results of the study showed that of the 4,446 students surveyed, 696 incidents of stalking were experienced by 581 (130.7 per 1,000) students, indicating that 13.1 percent of the women in the sample had been stalked at least once within one academic year. This count was reportedly not conclusive because 15 percent of the women (i.e. n=88/581*100) reported experiencing more than one stalking incident, while 12.7 percent experienced two incidents, and 2.3 percent experienced three or more incidents. It was also revealed in the study that where the stalker was known, there was a link to an established relationship or previously established relationship between the two as boyfriend or ex-boyfriend. It was further proved that one-quarter of the stalkers were classmates or coworkers.

The legal definition of stalking as "repeated pursuits carried out with the intent to harass or cause physical harm to the victim" theoretically classifies this crime into the rational-choice category. Implicitly, stalkers usually undergo strong emotional pressures that lure them into making the choice whether to stalk their victim or not. After properly weighing the benefits and costs of stalking, they would proceed with the act in full cognizance of the consequences. I am not however, ruling out the possibility that stalking may also be motivated by psychopathic influences in the offender. For instance, a mentally deranged man may purposelessly pursue a woman to the point of harming her. This is an example of an irrational-choice stalking. The difference between stalking perpetuated by a psychotic offender and that of a normal functional person, rests in the absence of the material ingredient, *mens rea* or *intent* in the act of the psychopathic stalker to make it a perfect crime. Some stalkers may be motivated simply by the desire to show masculine hegemony over the female victim, while others may be motivated by lust or the desire to satisfy their sexual passion.

Utilitarian desires may motivate stalking. This may either be to achieve something material (money or property) or to satisfy some sensual or sexual urge through the person being pursued. For instance, a former lover may want to revive their love relation or someone may be trying to establish a new love relationship. Stalking in itself may not really be criminal if evil intentions are not behind the motivation. What criminalizes stalking is not so much the simple act of pursuing someone as to its motive and sequel—harassing, harming, or even killing the victim, as has often been the case with most stalking incidents where the victim were females. Whatever the motive behind it, stalking is antisocial and an unacceptable attribute that should be eschewed early enough before it ever degenerates into evil.

In the following chapter, I have included a sample real-life case study that I carried out during my course work in the graduate school. My intention here is to provide some resource material to student advocates or those law enforcement officers (investigators) that may have to testify in a court of law as witness in a case they investigated. I have also added a sample case and review from a typical law school. All these are intended to enrich the knowledge of students and professional law enforcement officers reading this book on the processing of crimes from apprehension to judgment.

PART X

SAMPLE CRIMINAL CASE REVIEWS

i. DISTRICT COURT OF FAIRFAX, VIRGINIA:

Gregory v. Commonwealth of Virginia

Historical Background of the Case

Gregory v. Commonwealth of Virginia, reviewed in this course paper, is a murder case held in the Circuit Court of Virginia in Chesterfield County. The Commonwealth of Virginia (plaintiff) had sued Jason Wayne Gregory (defendant) for several offenses, including capital murder of James Michael Lambrecht. On July 20, 1998, following related trials and proceedings, Gregory was indicted on seven charges. After hearings on motions and trials from the lower courts to the Virginia State Appeal Court, the case was moved by certiorari[64] to the State Supreme Court of Virginia and decided on January 11, 2002. Presiding officials in this case included Leah A. Darron, assistant attorney general; Randolph A. Beales, attorney general, on brief for appellant; Steven D. Benjamin, on briefs for appellant; and Judge Donald W. Lemons. The Virginia State Supreme Court denied certiorari and, while affirming the ruling of the appellate court on the murder offenses, reversed the ruling on the burglary offenses.

---

[64]   A certiorari is a writ (an order) issued by a higher court to a lower court requesting for review of the record of a proceeding carried out by the lower court.

Legal Facts and Procedures

On December 31, 1997, James Michael Lambrecht (victim) was found by the police dead from gunshots in the head and lying in the backseat of a blue Ford Escort. According to a lead from Lambrecht's wife, Gregory, one of Lambrecht's marijuana clients, was suspected in connection with this murder. Police detectives picked up Jason Wayne Gregory (defendant), and after a brief interview with him, he was released on bail. On January 15, 1998, a burglary and vandalism of property worth $60,000 took place in the Redeemer Lutheran Church. Following another investigation based on a lead from a nearby convenience store worker as well as from an informant report, Gregory was found connected with the latter offenses.

On January 16, 1998, the police officially arrested Gregory and duly informed him of his Miranda rights,[65] which he waived both orally and in writing. In the ensuing investigation, Gregory confessed shooting Lambrecht and was arrested, officially charged with the murder of Lambrecht, and detained. On July 20, 1998, during pretrial and proceedings in which he was represented by three counsels appointed by the Circuit Court of Chesterfield County, Gregory was indicted by a grand jury of this court on seven charges namely: capital murder of James Lambrecht, use of a firearm in the commission of the murder of James Lambrecht, robbery of James Lambrecht, use of a firearm in the commission of robbery of James Lambrecht, breaking and entering the Redeemer Lutheran Church, grand larceny of property of Redeemer Lutheran Church, destruction of property of Redeemer Lutheran Church (vandalism). Gregory was represented by the following counsels: Wayne Morgan and Theodore Tondrowski in the burglary offenses and Steven Benjamin in the murder charge.

During a hearing on motion held on October 19, 1998, Gregory, in understanding with one of his counsels, Tondrowski, waived his right to speedy trial. During trial proceedings on the burglary offenses set on February 22, 1999, by the court, Gregory introduced a motion to suppress this charge with reasons that his statutory rights to speedy trial as per Code of

---

[65] The Miranda warnings are a statutory provision of the Sixth Amendment of the Constitution intended to protect the accused against self-incrimination during police interrogations. It requires the police officer to inform the suspect of his right to either respond to his questions or remain silent and use the services of his counsel to respond on his behalf.

Virginia sections 19.2-243[66] had been violated by his continued detention that exceeded five months following the determination of probable cause. Arguing against Gregory's suppression motion, the Commonwealth of Virginia contended that Gregory had officially waived his statutory rights to speedy trial as per Virginia State Code § 19.2-243(4) both orally and in writing and referred to his counsel (Tondrowski) that had consulted with Gregory and affirmed the waiver during hearing on motion held on October 19, 1998. Gregory was thus tried and convicted of burglary, vandalism, and grand larceny by the circuit court.

In a subsequent trial on the murder, robbery, and two counts of use of firearm to commit felony offenses, he was equally tried and convicted. Dissatisfied, he appealed against the two major offenses of burglary and murder charges. He argued that his Miranda rights were violated. The Virginia state court of appeals granted his appeal and reversed the ruling of the circuit court on the burglary charges while affirming the murder offenses. Ruling in reversal of the burglary offenses, the appellate court contended that the hearing on motion held on October 19, 1998, had not well addressed the burglary offenses since Morgan (Gregory's counsel) was absent. This absence, the court further argued, significantly affected whatever decision was arrived concerning the burglary charges and the speedy trial waiver. Consequently, Gregory's statutory rights to speedy trial were violated since he was not tried within the stipulated time. Regarding the murder offenses, the appellate court affirmed the circuit court's ruling on the murder charges.

Applying the precedence in *Miranda v. Arizona*, 384 US 436, 16 L. Ed. 2d 694, 86 S. Ct. 1602 (1966) and *Edwards v. Arizona*, 451 US 477, 68 L. Ed. 2d 378, 101 S. Ct. 1880 (1981), the court dismissed Gregory's argument that the police had violated his Miranda rights. The court held that the first interview was not custodial; besides, Gregory did not invoke his Miranda rights then. It further affirmed that since the police had advised him of these rights in the second interrogation, Gregory could not rightly assert that his Miranda rights were violated. Hence, the precedence (*Miranda v. Arizona* or *Edwards v. Arizona*) could not be applied in this case. While Gregory appealed against the court of appeals' ruling affirming conviction in the murder offenses, the Commonwealth of Virginia appealed against the appeal

---

[66] Code §19.2-243 states in part, "Where a general district court has found that there is probable cause to believe that the accused has committed a felony, the accused, if he is held continuously in custody thereafter, shall be forever discharged from prosecution for such offense if no trial is commenced in the circuit court within five months from the date such probable cause was found by the district court; and if the accused is not held in custody but has been recognized for his appearance in the circuit court to answer for such offense, he shall be forever discharged from prosecution."

court's reversal of the burglary convictions. It was at this juncture that the Virginia State Supreme Court by certiorari intervened in the case.

Opinions and Dissentions

Arguing on admissibility of the January 16, 1998, statements obtained by the police and presented as evidence against him in court, Gregory and his counsel maintained that Gregory did really invoke his Miranda rights and the need for counsel prior to any police interrogation, but the police did not heed his request and proceeded with their interrogation. They argued that the circuit court and the court of appeals' admission of evidence obtained during the January 4, 1998, interrogation violated the defendant's Fifth Amendment right against self-incrimination and his Sixth Amendment right to counsel. They further argued that admitting evidence also obtained from him during the January 16, 1998, interrogation by the police, the trial court, and the court of appeals clearly acted in violation of the precedence established in *Edwards*,[67] *McNeil v. Wisconsin*, 501 US. 171, 176, 115 L. Ed. 2d 158, 111 S. Ct. 2204 (1991).

The legal precedence established in *Edwards* states that if a suspect expresses the desire or the intent to deal with the police only through counsel prior to or during police interrogation, such interrogation must cease. But it may be resumed only if the suspect initiates the communication or conversation with the police. It is doubtlessly clear that the statutory Miranda warning provided by the Fifth Amendment of the Constitution is a prophylactic measure intended to protect the suspect against self-incrimination from the compelling pressures that are inherent in criminal interrogations. They further argued that any evidence obtained from the accused under such conditions was not of the defendant's volition but rather through the pressures induced by criminal interrogations. Consequently, any ensuing waiver of speedy trial rights was not offered voluntarily by the accused but rather imposed on him by the authorities.

In a dissenting opinion, Justice J. Scalia stated that the *Edwards* rule could only be applied in the circumstance where the suspect invoked his rights while still in custody. But Gregory was not in custody at the time, and as such the *Edwards* precedence could not be applied in this case. Regarding the Miranda warnings, J. Scalia also held that the police had given

---

[67] The *Edwards* precedence applied in *McNeil v. Wisconsin* states, "If the individual indicates in any manner, at any time prior to or during questioning, that he wishes to remain silent, the interrogation must cease . . . . If the individual states that he wants an attorney, the interrogation must cease until an attorney is present unless the accused himself initiates further communication, exchanges, or conversations with the police."

Gregory his Miranda warnings, which the latter had waived both orally and in writing during the January 16, 1998, interrogations. Moreover, in subsequent interrogations, Gregory had confessed to the murder offenses. In conclusion and on the strength of the above arguments, the Virginia State Supreme Court reversed the appellate court ruling on the burglary offenses, thereby reinstating the circuit court ruling. Meanwhile, in the murder offenses, this court similarly affirmed the circuit ruling. (This case was reviewed by the author of this book.)

ii. *Supreme Court of South Carolina v. James W. WORLEY,* Appellant No. 20123. 265 SC 551, 220 SE2d 242 Dec. 4, 1975

P. Lewis, Pitts, Jr., and W. Gaston Fairey, Columbia, for appellant. Atty. Gen. Daniel R. McLeod, Asst. Atty. Gen. Joseph R. Barker and Sol. James C. Anders, Columbia, for respondent. NESS, Justice:

This appeal involves the question of when a defendant who contends he escaped from lawful confinement due to inadequate medical treatment is entitled to have the affirmative defense of necessity submitted to the jury. In the instant case the trial judge refused to charge the defense of necessity. [Footnote omitted.] We affirm.

James Worley voluntarily left Richland County Prison Camp in June, 1972. He had opportunities to report to the authorities but failed to do so . . . . Worley was arrested in Florida and returned to South Carolina in July, 1974. He was convicted of escape and sentenced to one year imprisonment.

The living conditions at the Prison Camp were undesirable. Appellant contracted a severe case of poison ivy on his forearm. The poison ivy caused swelling and developed into a rash and open, running sores and appellant was given some calamine lotion by a camp official. On three occasions appellant requested to see a physician; these requests were denied . . . . Appellant, fearing he was in danger of serious bodily harm, departed the Camp. He went to Georgia and saw a doctor who successfully treated the condition by administering a shot and some medicine.

Courts have been reluctant to consider a defense of necessity in escape cases based on prison conditions or lack of medical treatment. Sound reasons underlie this policy. It is not the prerogative of prisoners to decide escape is justified. Legal channels are available to contest inadequate treatment. If the defense of necessity was commonly available, the number of escape attempts would increase . . . . Escapes would be encouraged even though they are dangerous to prison guards, officials and the public and are disruptive of prison routine. See State v. Palmer, 6 Terry 308, 45 Del. 308, 72 A.2d 442 (1950).

[However,] . . . [i]f a prisoner is in need of emergency medical treatment to avoid death or immediate, serious permanent bodily injury, he may have a defense of necessity submitted to the jury. Certain minimum conditions are set forth as guidelines which must be satisfied before this defense is available. (1) The prisoner must have informed prison officials of the condition . . . and have been denied professional medical care; (2) There must not be time to resort to the courts; (3) The escape must be without use or threat of use of force; (4) The escapee must promptly seek professional medical treatment; (5) The treating physician . . . must testify the prisoner was actually in danger of death or immediate serious permanent bodily injury unless the prisoner was given prompt professional medical treatment; (6) After seeing the physician, the prisoner must immediately surrender himself to the authorities.

. . . .

The appellant remained at large for two years and for this reason alone his plea of necessity was properly rejected by the court.

The limitations we have placed on the availability of this defense are necessarily rigid . . . . The demands of public safety and efficient running of the prison system must be balanced against the potentially meritorious assertion of a prisoner. The standard we have established attempts to accommodate both interests. It affords a prisoner who finds himself in unusual and dire circumstances a reasonable alternative to death or serious bodily injury. Likewise, it protects against assertions by those prisoners who would endanger prison life and public safety by escaping and fabricate charges of inhuman treatment or neglect as an afterthought to their flight from justice.

Affirmed.

LEWIS, C.J., and LITTLEJOHN, RHODES and GREGORY, JJ., concur.

SAMPLE BRIEF

Case Name: *State v. Worley*, 265 S.C. 551, 220 S.E.2d 242 (1975)

Facts: James Worley, the Defendant in this case, was an inmate at Richland County Prison camp in 1972. While in the camp, he contracted a severe case of poison ivy. He asked three times to see a doctor, but was not allowed to do so. He was given calamine lotion as treatment. The Defendant voluntarily left the Camp and went to Georgia, where he was treated by a doctor. He was arrested two years later in Florida and charged with the crime of escape from lawful confinement.

Procedural History: The Defendant was convicted in South Carolina state court of escape and argued at trial that his escape was justified because of inadequate medical treatment at the prison camp. The trial judge refused to allow the Defendant to present the affirmative defense of necessity to the jury. The Defendant appeals his conviction on the basis that the trial judge should have charged the jury with the necessity defense.

Issue: Did the trial court err in failing to allow the jury to consider a necessity defense in an escape from lawful confinement case where the Defendant left a prison camp due to inadequate medical treatment and promptly sought proper medical treatment, but failed to report to authorities during the two years that followed?

Holding (and Judgment): No, the trial court did not err in withdrawing the necessity defense from the jury's consideration because the Defendant remained at large, without reporting to authorities, for two years after he left the prison camp. (Affirmed.)

Pre-Existing Rules: The case does not cite the statute that criminalizes escape from lawful confinement, but presumably such a statute exists. The necessity defense had apparently not been recognized by South Carolina courts in this context, so the criteria set forth in this case define a new affirmative defense.

Reasoning: The court reasoned that the defense of necessity must be available only in limited situations because legal channels exist to address problems with medical treatment, and, therefore, prisoners should not be the ones to decide when escape is justified. The court observed that escapes are "dangerous to prison guards, officials and the public and are disruptive of prison routine." The court set forth six criteria that must be satisfied in order for the necessity defense to be available to a prisoner charged with escape: 1) the prisoner must have informed prison officials of the problem and been denied medical treatment; 2) there must not be time for a court to address the problem; 3) the escape must not involve force or threat of force; 4) the escapee must promptly seek medical care; 5) the treating doctor must agree that the prisoner was in danger of death or "immediate serious permanent" bodily harm absent prompt medical care; and 6) the prisoner must report to authorities immediately after receiving medical care. Because the 6th criterion was not satisfied by the Defendant, the court held that the trial court did not err in withholding the necessity defense. 7

Dissents/Concurrences: None.

My Comments: The fact that the Defendant didn't turn himself in for two years was enough grounds for the court to affirm his conviction, but there also seems to be a question of whether poison ivy puts a prisoner in sufficient danger of death or serious, permanent bodily harm to satisfy the fifth criterion. Also, a case of poison ivy may lack the urgency apparently required by the second criterion. But the court did not need to address either of these issues because the Defendant's failure to fulfill the sixth criterion, alone, automatically made the defense unavailable to him. As a result, it's unclear how the fifth and second criteria might impact the outcome of a different case. (Sample extract from a law school.)

iii. UNITED STATES V. FREED

United States v. Freed, 401 US 601, 91 S. Ct. 1112, 28 L. Ed. 2d 356 (1971).

Facts: Freed (D) and other defendants were indicted for possession of unregistered hand grenades in violation of a federal law, that made it unlawful for anyone to "receive or possess a firearm which is not registered to him." Freed claimed that he did not know of the obligation to register the hand grenades, and therefore did not have the required specific intent to possess the unregistered weapons. The district court dismissed the indictments on the grounds that the failure to allege scienter (knowingly) for the crime was violative of due process and the government appealed.

Issue: Is a statute that imposes criminal liability for possession of unregistered weapons, without regards to whether a defendant knew of the requirement to register, unconstitutional for lack of due process?

Holding and Rule (Douglass): No. The imposition of criminal liability for possession of unregistered weapons, without regard to whether a defendant knew of the requirement to register, is not violative of due process.

The federal law in question prohibits an individual from receiving or possessing a firearm not registered to him. This statute is a regulatory measure made in the interest of public safety and is premised on the idea that possession of hand grenades in itself is not a safe, innocent activity. A reasonable person would likely suspect that possession of hand grenades is illegal. Since this activity is not innocent and since the statute is regulatory, no specific intent is required. The defendant's mere knowledge that he possessed the unregistered hand grenades is sufficient to sustain a conviction.

Disposition: Reversed.

Concurring (Brennan): The mens rea requirement is a rule, rather than an exception, to Anglo-American law. This requirement is universal and persistent and is generally required. A clear congressional intent is needed to discard the mens rea requirement. I think it is reasonable to conclude that Congress dispensed with the requirement of intent in this case.

Notes: The court distinguishes between activity that would seem unlawful to the average citizen and activity that is in itself harmless. For example—Lambert v. California involved a law that made it a crime to remain in Los Angeles for more than five days without registering if a person had been convicted of a felony. That law was held unconstitutional because one's presence in Los Angeles is not in itself something that would seem to be unlawful to the average citizen.

(See *DPP v. Majewski* for a British criminal law case brief in which the House of Lords held that voluntary intoxication is not a valid defense to general intent crimes.)

BIBLIOGRAPHY

Allan Wright, Policing: <u>An Introduction to Concepts and Practice</u>.

<u>American Criminal Law Review</u>, Fall 2002 v39 i4 p1501 (33). The USA-PATRIOT Act and the American response to terror: "can we protect civil

Arthur Burnett, <u>American Criminal Law Review</u>, summer 1994 v31

Barry Rosenfeld, <u>Criminal Justice and Behavior</u>, Feb 2004 v31 i1 P9 (28): Violence risk factors in stalking and obsessional harassment: a review and preliminary meta-analysis.

Bruce L. Benson, Brent D. Mast and David W. Rasmussen N, <u>Applied Economics</u>, Feb 20, 2000, v32 i3 p357, "Can police deter drunk driving?"

Carl Klockers and Steven Mastrofski, 1991 <u>Thinking about Police</u>; Contemporary Readings

Cassia Spohn and David Holleran. <u>Criminology</u>, May 2002 v40 i2 p329 (29)." The effect of imprisonment on recidivism rates of felony"

Cullen, Ball and al, <u>Criminology Theory</u>, 2002, Sage Publications Inc. Thousand Oaks, US expound on the "rational choice theory" that contends that every criminal weighs the benefits and risks of his actions before embarking on any crime.

<u>Federal Protective Service Security Guard Information Manual</u> (SGIM), July 2006 Revision— by The Department of Homeland Security.

Fisher, Cullen and Turner, <u>Criminology and Public Policy</u>. Columbus. March, 2002 vol. 1.

Frank and Hagan, 1986. <u>Introduction to Criminology</u>: Theories, Methods and Criminal Behavior, Library of Congress Publication. Applied Theories as opposed to Pure Theories, make practical explanations that may guide existing policies in any research undertaking.

Jack Katz, 1988. <u>Seductions of Crime</u>: "A chilling exploration of the criminal mind from juvenile delinquency to cold-blooded murder," Basic Book, US.

James Q. Wilson and Joan Petersilia: <u>Crime: Public policies for Crime control</u>, CS Press Oakland CA.

James Q. Wilson and Joan Petersilia: <u>Crime: Public policies for Crime control</u>, CS Press Oakland CA liberties after September 11?"

Michele Cotton, <u>American Criminal Law Review</u>, Fall 2000 v37 i4 p1313. "Back with a vengeance"

Penny Dick;2005 <u>Dirty work designations</u>: How police officers account for their use of coercive force; Sheffield University Management School, UK.

FBI'S Uniform Crime Reports.

Human Trafficking and the Child Protection Compact Act of 2009

By Louis Klarevas and Christine Buckley.

Peter J.Benekos and Alida Merlo, Three Strikes and you're Out! The political Sentencing Game.

Peter K. Manning, <u>American Behavioral Scientist,</u>" May-June 1993 v36 n5 p (639) "The Preventive Conceit"

Peter W. Greenwood. "Juvenile Crime and Juvenile Justice" page 89-92. James Q. Wilson and Joan Petersilia: <u>Crime: Public policies for Crime control</u>, CS Press Oakland CA.

Samenow, 1985. <u>Inside the Criminal Mind</u> is here making a reference to his free will concept of crime (Choice Theory). The criminal he believes, makes the choice to commit crimes.

Samuel walker. Sense and Non Sense about crime and Drugs, Wadsworth, 2001, page 113

Samuel walker. <u>Sense and Non-sense about Crime and Drug</u>, 2001 Wadsworth, pages 18-21

Samuel walker: <u>Sense and Non-sense about Crime and Drug</u>, 2001 Wadsworth, "Putting Severity of Punishment back in the deterrence package"

Silvia M. Mendes and Michael D. McDonald, <u>Policy Studies Journal</u>, Winter 2001 v29 i4 p588 (23).

Stephen W. Baron and Leslie W. Kennedy <u>Canadian Journal of Criminology</u>, Jan 1998 v40 n1 p27-60. Deterrence and Homeless Male Street Youths. (Canada)

Steven D. Levitt, <u>Economic Inquiry</u> 1998, "Why Do Increased Arrest Rates Appear to Reduce Crime: Deterrence, Incapacitation, or Measurement Error?"

<u>The Journal of Criminal Law and Criminology</u>, Capital Punishment and Deterrence: Conflicting Evidence, 1983 Northwestern University School of Law. Vol. 74, No. 3

Urban Politics, Crime Rates, and Police Strength; Thomas D. Stucky; 2005, LFB Scholarly Publishing LLC.

Valerie Wright; "Deterrence in Criminal Justice": Evaluating Certainty vs. Severity of Punishment; 2010 Washington DC

WEBSITES

"Delivering data: Let's end up with poverty (for our own sake!)." Delivering data. N.p, n.d. Web. 3 Feb. 2012. <http://www.deliveringdata.com/2011/10/lets-end-up-with-poverty-for-our—own.html>.

"Memorial service Thursday for 48th remembrance of Birmingham church bombing | Alabama's 13." *Birmingham, Tuscaloosa, & Anniston, Alabama News, Weather, & Tornado Coverage | Alabama's 13.* N.p., n.d. Web. 13 Apr. 2012. <http://www2.alabamas13.com/news/2011/sep/15/memorial-service-thursday-48th-remembrance-birming-ar-2413569/>.

"Miranda Warning (law Enforcement)." *Encyclopedia Britannica Online.* Encyclopedia Britannica, n.d. Web. 29 Oct. 2012. <http://www.britannica.com/EBchecked/topic/384939/Miranda-warning>.

"Ojp." Http://www.ojp.usdoj.gov/bjs/glance/incrt.htm. N.p., n.d. Web.

"Photo Galleries | Martin Luther King | Seattle Times Newspaper." *The Seattle Times | Seattle Times Newspaper.* N.p., n.d. Web. 13 Apr. 2012. <http://seattletimes.nwsource.com/special/mlk/king/photogalleries

"Violence Prevention Home Page|Injury|CDC." *Centers for Disease Control and Prevention.* N.p., n.d. Web. 7 May 2013. <http://www.cdc.gov/violenceprevention/index.

"Welcome to the United States Department of Justice." *Welcome to the United States Department of Justice.* N.p., n.d. Web. 28 Oct. 2013. <http://www.justice.gov/>.*Http://www.stun-cuff.com/members/1558099/uploaded/Latest_Bro.pdf.* N.p., n.d. Web.

"What Is a Gang? Definitions | National Institute of Justice." *National Institute of Justice: Criminal Justice Research, Development and Evaluation.* N.p., n.d. Web. 14 Apr. 2012. <http://www.nij.gov/nij/topics/crime/gangs-organized/gangs/definitions.htm>.

"What Is a Gang? Definitions." *National Institute of Justice.* N.p., n.d. Web. 28 Oct. 2013. <http://www.nij.gov/nij/topics/crime/gangs-organized/gangs/definitions.htm>.

"What is an Environmental Crime? | Criminal Enforcement | Compliance and Enforcement | US EPA." *US Environmental Protection Agency.* N.p., n.d. Web. 14 Apr. 2012. <http://www.epa.gov/compliance/criminal/investigations/environmentalcrime.html>.

"Why Do Increased Arrest Rates Appear to Reduce Crime: Deterrence, Incapacitation, or Measurement Error?" *Why Do Increased Arrest Rates Appear to Reduce Crime: Deterrence, Incapacitation, or Measurement Error?* Ideas, n.d. Web. 29 Oct. 2012. <http://ideas.repec.org/p/nbr/nberwo/5268.html>.

Age. (n.d.). U. S. Crime Statistics Total and by State 1960-2009. The Disaster Center—Home Page. Retrieved August 14, 2011, from http://www.disastercenter.com/crime/

Bureau of Justice Statistics Incarceration Rate Trends Chart. (n.d.). Bureau of Justice Statistics (BJS). Retrieved August 14, 2011, from http://bjs.ojp.usdoj.gov/content/glance/incrt.cfm

Bureau of Justice Statistics Violent Crime Rate Trends. (n.d.). Bureau of Justice Statistics (BJS). Retrieved August 14, 2011, from http://bjs.ojp.usdoj.gov/content/glance/viort.cfm

By Dee-Ann Durbin/Associated Press

Centers for Disease Control and Prevention. Centers for Disease Control and Prevention, 15 Aug. 2012. Web. 29 Oct. 2012. <http://www.cdc.gov/ncipc/dvp/fivpt.>.

"Equilibrium is society's best medicine . . ." *Christlike.html.* N.p., n.d. Web. 3 Feb. 2012. <http://liberalslikechrist.org/about/socialequilibrium.html>.

FBI—Crime in the U.S. 2011. *FBI—Homepage.* Retrieved October 15, 2013, from http://www.fbi.gov/about-us/cjis/ucr/crime-in-the-u.s/2011/crime-in-the-u.s.-2011

Figure 1: Homicide rates per 100,000 populations in Texas, New York, and California.

Fisher, M. (n.d.). What makes America's gun culture totally unique in the world, in four charts. *The Washington Post: National, World & D.C. Area News and Headlines—The Washington Post.* Retrieved October 15, 2013, from http://www.washingtonpost.com/blogs/worldviews/wp/2012/12/15/what-makes-americas-gun-culture-totally-unique-in-the-world-as-demonstrated-in-four-charts/

http://human-trafficking-wiki.wikispaces.com/

http://www.fbi.gov/about-us/cjis/ucr/crime-in-the-u.s/2011/crime-in-the-u.s.-2011/tables/expanded-homicide-data-table-1

http://www.fbi.gov/about-us/cjis/ucr/crime-in-the-u.s/2011/crime-in-the-u.s.-2011/violent-crime/violent-crime

FBI." *FBI.* 17 Mar. 2010. Web. 23 Nov. 2013. <http://www.fbi.gov/about-us/investigate/civilrights>.

Http://www.ncjrs.org/txtfiles/169592.txt. N.p., n.d. Web.

Http://www.stlouis.missouri.org/enterprise/about/crime.html. St. louis.missouri.org, n.d. Web. 29 Oct. 2012. <http://www.stlouis.missouri.org/enterprise/about/crime.html>.

Human Trafficking. (n.d.). *U.S. Immigration and Customs Enforcement.* Retrieved October 15, 2013, from http://www.ice.gov/human-trafficking

Human Trafficking." *Human Trafficking.* ICE.gov, n.d. Web. 28 Oct. 2012. <http://www.ice. gov/human-trafficking/

Karl Marx Capitalism Marxism Critique Of Capitalism. Rep. N.p., n.d. Web. 29 Oct. 2012. <http://www.economictheories.org/2008/07/karl-marx-capitalism-marxism-critique.html>.

Morris systems. Advertisement.—*FOR SALE.* N.p., n.d. Web. 29 Oct. 2012. <http://www. morrissystems.com/dvrs.htm>.

Morris systems. Advertisement.—*FOR SALE.* N.p., n.d. Web. 29 Oct. 2012. <http://www. morrissystems.com/cameras.htm>.

"The Dashboard Spy." *The Dashboard Spy.* N.p., n.d. Web. 19 Nov. 2013. <http:// dashboardspy.wordpress.com/2006/04/19/crime-analysis-dashboard-using-mapping-and-enterprise-dashboard-techniques-to-fight->.

Ojp, n.d. Web. <http://www.ojp.usdoj.gov/bjs/glance/viort.htm>.

Soc 3: Social Problems—Sex Trade and Human Trafficking." Social problems ucd, n.d. Web. 29 Oct. 2012. <http://socialproblemsucd.wikispaces.com/Sex Trade and Human Trafficking>.

The Facilitators | Polaris Project | Combating Human Trafficking and Modern-day Slavery. Rep. Polaris project, n.d. Web. 29 Oct. 2012. <http://www.polarisproject.org/ human-trafficking/overview/the-facilitators>.

US. Gao. N.p., n.d. Web. 29 Oct. 2012. <http://www.gao.gov/atext/d03144.txt>.

US. Ncip. Centers for Disease Control and Prevention. Centers for Disease Control and Prevention, n.d. Web. 29 Oct. 2012. <http://www.cdc.gov/ncipc>.

THE AUTHOR

Nubong Thomas Asongwe was born in Bambili Village, NW province of Cameroon, about 1959 (birth registry inexistent then). He attended St. Francis Primary School Ntsewih, Bambili. In September 1969 he was admitted into the Government Bilingual Secondary School, Yaoundé (College Bilingue d'Application de l'Ecole Normale Superieure) where he completed in 1975 and went to CCAST Bambili. On graduation with a pass at the GCE Advanced Levels in 1977, he accepted the offer to teach English Literature and French for two years in PCC Mankon, Bamenda. He later enrolled  in the University of Yaoundé, Cameroon (and partly in Universite de Creteil, Paris XII, Val-de-Marne France through an exchange program). He obtained a BA degree in letters in June 1982. He accepted a government job offer and taught English Language and Literature for a year in Lycee D'Ombessa, Mbam Division in the Center Province. In 1983 he was admitted into the National Higher School for Prison Administration (NHSPA), Buea.

On completion in 1985, he worked in various positions as corrections administrator for the Cameroon government. In October 1999 he moved to USA for further studies. He accepted a job offer as deputy sheriff in Cleveland County Sheriff Department in Norman, Oklahoma, while he enrolled and read Computer Technology and Networking in Moore/Norman Technical College. In 2002 he earned admission into the graduate school in George Mason University, Fairfax, Virginia where he read Public Administration with a major in Administration of Justice (Management of Law Enforcement Services). He graduated in 2006

141

with an MA in public administration and a postgraduate diploma in Administration of Justice (in tandem). Concurrently with studies, he worked as senior staff with Securitas Inc. USA, an international security firm. He is currently a protective service officer (PSO) contracted to the USA Federal Protective Service, a unit of the federal police under the Department of Homeland Security (DHS). Nubong is married to Na-Nde Susana, and both are blessed parents of four girls, a son, and two grandsons.